Super Cheap Paris Travel Guide

"Paris is not a city; it's a world." – King Francis I

Our Mission

Did you know you can fly on a private jet for $500? Yes, a fully private jet. Complete with flutes of champagne and reclinable creamy leather seats. Your average billionaire spends $20,00 on the exact same flight. You can get it for $500 when you book private jet empty leg flights. Amazed? Don't be. This is just one of thousands of ways you can travel luxuriously on a budget.

When our brain hears the word "budget" it hears deprivation, suffering, agony, even depression. But budget travel need not be synonymous with hostels and pack lunches. You can enjoy an incredible and luxurious trip to Paris on a budget, just like you can enjoy a private jet flight for 10% of the normal cost when you know how. The past years have shown us travel is a gift we must cherish. We believe strongly that this gift is best enjoyed on a budget. Together with thrifty locals, we have funneled our passion for travel bargains into Super Cheap Paris.

Our passion is finding travel bargains. This doesn't mean doing less or sleeping in hostels. Someone who spends A LOT on travel hasn't planned or wants to spend their money. We promise you that with a bit of planning, you can experience a luxury trip to Paris on a budget.

Traveling need not be expensive; Travel guides, Travel agents, Travel bloggers and influencers often show you overpriced accommodation, restaurants and big-ticket attractions because they earn commission from your "we're on vacation" mentality, which often leads to reckless spending. Our mission is to teach you how to enjoy more for less and get the best value from every dollar you spend in Paris.

Taking a trip to Paris is not just an outer journey, it's an inner one. Budget travel brings you closer to locals, culture and authenticity; which makes your inner journey more fulfilling.
Super Cheap Paris will save you 1000 times what you paid for it while teaching you local tips and tricks. We have formulated a

system to pass on to you, so you can enjoy a luxurious trip to Paris without the nightmare credit card bill.

Our mission is to dispel myths, save you tons of money, give you the local tips and tricks and help you find experiences in Paris that will flash before your eyes when you come to take your last breath on this beautiful earth.

Who this book is for and why anyone can enjoy budget travel

There is a big difference between being cheap and frugal. Who doesn't like to spend money on beautiful experiences?

Over 20 years of travel has taught me I could have a 20 cent experience that will stir my soul more than a $100 one. Of course, sometimes the reverse is true, my point is, spending money on travel is the best investment you can make but it doesn't have to be at levels set by hotels and attractions with massive ad spends and influencers who are paid small fortunes to get you to buy into something you could have for a fraction of the cost.

This book is for those who want to have the cold hard budget busting facts to hand (which is why we've included so many one page charts, which you can use as a quick reference), but otherwise, the book provides plenty of tips to help you shape your own Paris experience.

We have designed these travel guides to give you a unique planning tool to experience an unforgettable trip without spending the ascribed tourist budget.

This guide focuses on Paris's unbelievable bargains. Of course, there is little value in traveling to Paris and not experiencing everything it has to offer. Where possible, we've included cheap workarounds or listed the experience in the Loved but Costly section.

When it comes to FUN budget travel, it's all about what you know. You can have all the feels without most of the bills. A few days spent planning can save you thousands. Luckily, we've done the planning for you, so you can distill the information in minutes not days, leaving you to focus on what matters: immersing yourself in the sights, sounds and smells of Paris, meeting awesome new people and feeling relaxed and happy. I sincerely hope our tips will bring you great joy at a fraction of the price you expected.

So, grab a cup of tea or coffee, put your feet up and relax; you're about to enter the world of enjoying Paris on the cheap. Oh, and don't forget a biscuit. You need energy to plan a trip of a lifetime on a budget.

Super Cheap Paris is <u>not</u> for travellers with the following needs:

1. You require a book with detailed offline travel maps. Super Cheap Insider Guides are best used with Google Maps - download before you travel to make the most of your time and money.
2. You would like thousands of accommodation, food and attraction recommendations; by definition, cheapest is often singular. We only include maximum value recommendations. We purposively leave out over-priced attractions when there is no workaround.
3. You would like detailed write-ups about hotels/Airbnbs/ Restaurants. We are bargain hunters first and foremost. We dedicate our time to finding the best deals, not writing flowery language about their interiors. Plus, things change. If I had a pound for every time I'd read a Lonely Planet description only to find the place totally different, I would be a rich man. Always look at online reviews for the latest up-to-date information.

If you want to save A LOT of money while comfortably enjoying an unforgettable trip to Paris, minus the marketing, hype, scams and tourist traps read on.

Redefining Super Cheap

The value you get out of Super Cheap Paris is not based on what you paid for it; it's based on what you do with it. You can only do great things with it if you believe saving money is worth your time. Charging things to your credit card and thinking 'oh I'll pay it off when I get home' is something you won't be tempted to do if you change your beliefs now. Think about what you associate with the word cheap, because you make your beliefs and your beliefs make you.

I grew up thinking you had to spend more than you could afford to have a good time traveling. Now I've visited 190 countries, I know nothing is further from the truth. Before you embark upon reading our specific tips for Paris think about your associations with the word cheap.

Here are the dictionary definitions of cheap:

- Costing very little; relatively low in price; inexpensive: a cheap dress.
- costing little labor or trouble: Words are cheap.
- charging low prices: a very cheap store.
- Of little account; of small value; mean; shoddy: Cheap conduct; cheap workmanship.
- Embarrassed; sheepish: He felt cheap about his mistake.
- Stingy; miserly: He's too cheap to buy his own brother a cup of coffee.

Three out of six definitions have extremely negative connotations. The 'super cheap' we're talking about in this book is not shoddy, embarrassed, or stingy.
We added the super to reinforce our message. Super's dictionary definition stands for 'a super quality'. Super Cheap stands for enjoying the best on the lowest budget. Question other people's definitions of cheap so you're not blinded to possibilities, poten-

tial, and prosperity. Here are some new associations to consider forging:

Shoddy

Cheap stuff doesn't last is an adage marketing companies have drilled into consumers. However, by asking vendors the right questions cheap doesn't mean something won't last. I had a $10 backpack last for 8 years and a $100 suitcase bust on the first journey.

A study out of San Francisco University found that people who spent money on experiences rather than things were happier. Memories last forever, not things, even expensive things. And as we will show you during this guide, you don't need to pay to create glorious memories.[1]

Embarrassed

I have friends who routinely pay more to vendors because they think their money is putting food on this person's table. Paradoxically, Cuban doctors are driving taxis because they earn more money; it's not always a good thing for the place you're visiting to pay more and can cause unwanted distortion in their culture - Airbnb pushing out renters is an obvious example. Think carefully about whether the extra money is helping people or incentivising greed.

Stingy

Cheap can be eco-friendly. Buying thrift clothes is cheap, but you also help the Earth. Many travellers are often disillusioned by the reality of traveling since the places on our bucket-lists are over-crowded. Cheap can take you away from the crowds. You can find balance and harmony being cheap. "Remember a journey is

---

[1] Paulina Pchelin & Ryan T. Howell (2014) The hidden cost of value-seeking: People do not accurately forecast the economic benefits of experiential purchases, The Journal of Positive Psychology, 9:4, 322-334, DOI: 10.1080/17439760.2014.898316

best measured in friends, rather than miles." – Tim Cahill. And making friends is free!

A recent survey by Credit Karma found 50% of Millennials and Gen Z get into debt traveling. **Please don't allow credit card debt to be an unwanted souvenir you take home.** As you will see from this book, there's so much you can enjoy in Paris for free, some many unique bargains and so many ways to save money! You just need to want to!

Discover Paris

Known as the "City of Light" or the "City of Love," the streets of Paris overflow with culture, art, beauty, and history.Paris is everything you've imagined and more - a global trendsetter, a market leader, a thousand year old cultural capital strewn with instantly recognisable landmarks, glorious museums, cultural treasures and the best people watching.

You'll find monuments that represent centuries of history and architectural achievements, as well as parks and green spaces that make the city feel more open and welcoming than the Parisan's.

Paris is a city of firsts: in 1915 during World War I a fraction of the Parisian army was the first to use camouflage, which comes from the French verb "to make up for the stage." The first public screening of a movie was held here in 1895. They used their invention "the cinématographe" to show 10 films of about 50 seconds each. And of course, fashion was born in Paris; the wide boulevards gave birth to the first catwalks in the 19th century.

Paris was founded at the end of the 3rd century BC by the Gauls who were called Parisii. The Romans invaded and renamed the City "Lutetia." After almost two thousand years of tumultuous history spanning the French revolution, Napoleon and Hitler's infamous photo in front of the Eiffel tower, the modern-day city is still filled with elegant Parisians lounging outside cafés drinking coffee living its Motto: 'Liberté, Egalité, Fraternité' (translation: Liberty, Equality, Fraternity).

Everywhere you look in Paris there is another building to photograph. There are 6,100 rues – or streets – to snap in Paris. Stroll the boulevards, shop till you drop, marvel at the Eiffel Tower (intended to stand for 20 years after being built in1889) flop riverside with a block of brie and watch the world buzz by from a streetside cafe. Savour it all.

Whether you are looking for a romantic escape or an exciting history lesson, Paris offers a little bit of everything. You can spend days sightseeing in the parks or indulging in local gastronomic bliss. You can enjoy a glass of wine while people-watching in a quaint streetside cafe.

As the most visited city in the world, it comes as no surprise that Paris is also one of the most expensive. According to a recent Economist Intelligence Unit (EIU) survey, Paris is the most expensive city to live in. In fact, living in Paris is nearly 7 percent more expensive than living in New York. but take heart. The trick to keeping your trip cheap but incredible is to get off the tourist track and find the local deals. If you follow the advice in this guide you could definitely get away with spending about $60 a day per person including luxury accommodation.

Some of Paris' Best Bargains

Take a custom tour of Paris for free

 A little known hack to get a free custom tour of Paris is booking with Paris Greeters. They arrange free tours for one to six visitors with local volunteers. Submit your request online at www.greeters.paris specifying your language, interests and preferred date and time.

MORE FREE TOURS

- From April to October the City of Paris organizes free guided tours of the Jardin sauvage Saint-Vincent in the 18th arrondissement. The tour starts at 3:30pm, and is led by park wardens.
- Another impressive free tour is the Discover Walks tour of Paris' Marais district. You'll walk through some of the oldest aristocratic neighborhoods in the city while learning about the history of the district. You'll also get a taste of Parisian life and learn about the best spots to get a drink, shop, and dine. The Discover Walks free tour is the most comprehensive and longest of the free guided tours of Paris. It covers over 2,000 years of Parisian history while covering the best sites to see in the city. You'll also get a sneak peak at some of the city's most interesting landmarks, like the fabled Saint Germain des Pres church and the Palais Royal.

Get an incredible free view of the Eiffel Tower

Go to Quai Branly museum rooftop restaurant where you can sip a cheap coffee and get an incredible view of the Eiffel Tower. The Museum is free to enter.

Visit Musée d'Orsay cheaply

Located on the left bank of the Seine, Muse dOrsay is home to the largest collection of Impressionist art in the world by artists like Claude Monet and Vincent Van Gogh. Muse dOrsay is also home to the world famous Bal du Moulin de la Galette, a painting by Renoir.

If you're keen to visit Musée d'Orsay, go after 6pm on Thursdays, its 40% cheaper and less crowded. Access to the museum is free for all on the 1st Sunday of every month. Also on Thursdays visitors can also enjoy the Summer Terrace, which is located high above the city and offers a great view of the Louvre.

Take in a free performance

Visit Eglise de la Madeleine. The Madeleine Church was designed in its present form as a temple to the glory of Napoleon's army. Today you can experience free organ recitals, chamber concerts, and choral performances inside this Beautiful church. Visit http://www.eglise-lamadeleine.com/
 for an up-to-date schedule.

Visit the thrones French kings were once crowned upon for free

The Cabinet des Médailles et Monnaies on rue de Richelieu is an eclectic collection of antiques, jewellery and the 7th century Dagobert's Throne, on which French kings were once crowned. It is also the oldest museum in France and after 3pm, it's free to enter.

Eat at Michelin-starred restaurant

Seven of the ten most affordable Michelin star restaurants in Europe are located in France. In Paris, **Auguste** offers a classic menu of traditional French dishes. The restaurant's location is also excellent with views of the Eiffel Tower. The restaurant has a clean, white and modern interior and the Lunch menu is a steal for a one-star Michelin star restaurant at just €39!

Indulge in Happy hours

At La Cordonnerie pints and bottles of French beer are just €3 during happy hour (5pm to 8.30pm).

Address: 142 Rue Saint-Denis

How to Enjoy ALLO-CATING Money in Paris

'Money's greatest intrinsic value—and this can't be overstated—is its ability to give you control over your time.' - Morgan Housel

Notice I have titled the chapter how to enjoy allocating money in Paris. I'll use saving and allocating interchangeably in the book, but since most people associate saving to feel like a turtleneck, that's too tight, I've chosen to use wealth language. Rich people don't save. They allocate. What's the difference? Saving can feel like something you don't want or wish to do and allocating has your personal will attached to it.

And on that note, it would be helpful if you considered removing the following words and phrase from your vocabulary for planning and enjoying your Paris trip:

- Wish

- Want

- Maybe someday

These words are part of poverty language. Language is a dominant source of creation. Use it to your advantage. You don't have to wish, want or say maybe someday to Paris. You can enjoy the same things millionaires enjoy in Paris without the huge spend.

'People don't like to be sold-but they love to buy.' - Jeffrey Gitomer.

Every good salesperson who understands the quote above places obstacles in the way of their clients' buying. Companies create waiting lists, restaurants pay people to queue outside in order to create demand. People reason if something is so in demand, it must be worth having but that's often just marketing. Take this sales maxim 'People don't like to be sold-but they love to buy and flip it on its head to allocate your money in Paris on things YOU desire. You love to spend and hate to be sold. That means when something comes your way, it's not 'I can't afford it,' it's 'I don't want it' or maybe 'I don't want it right now'.

Saving money doesn't mean never buying a latte, never taking a taxi, never taking vacations (of course, you bought this book). Only you get to decide on how you spend and on what. Not an advice columnist who thinks you can buy a house if you never eat avocado toast again.

I love what Kate Northrup says about affording something: "If you really wanted it you would figure out a way to get it. If it were that VALUABLE to you, you would make it happen."

I believe if you master the art of allocating money to bargains, it can feel even better than spending it! Bold claim, I know. But here's the truth: Money gives you freedom and options. The more you keep in your account and or invested the more freedom and options you'll have. The principal reason you should save and allocate money is TO BE FREE! Remember, a trip's main purpose is relaxation, rest and enjoyment, aka to feel free.

When you talk to most people about saving money on vacation. They grimace. How awful they proclaim not to go wild on your vacation. If you can't get into a ton of debt enjoying your once-in-a-lifetime vacation, when can you?

When you spend money 'theres's a sudden rush of dopamine which vanishes once the transaction is complete. What happens in the brain when you save money? It increases feelings of security and peace. You don't need to stress life's uncertainties. And having a greater sense of peace can actually help you save more money.' Stressed out people make impulsive financial choices, calm people don't.'

The secret to enjoying saving money on vacation is very simple: never save money from a position of lack. Don't think 'I wish I could afford that'. Choose not to be marketed to. Choose not to consume at a price others set. Don't save money from the flawed premise you don't have enough. Don't waste your time living in the box that society has created, which says saving money on vacation means sacrifice. It doesn't.

Traveling to Paris can be an expensive endeavor if you don't approach it with a plan, but you have this book which is packed with tips. The biggest other asset is your perspective.

How to feel RICH in Paris

You don't need millions in your bank to feel rich. "Researchers have pooled data on the relationship between money and emotions from more than 1.6 million people across 162 countries and found that wealthier people feel more positive "self-regard emotions" such as confidence, pride and determination."

Here are things to see, do and taste in Paris, that will have you overflowing with gratitude for your luxury trip to Paris.

- Achieving a Michelin Star rating is the most coveted accolade for restaurants but those that obtain a Michelin Star are synonymous with high cost, but in Paris there are restaurants with Michelin-stars offering lunch menus for 50 Euros or less! If you want to taste the finest seasonal local dishes while dining in pure luxury, visit Contraste, L'Innocence or Jacques Faussat to indulge in an unforgettable treat. If fine dining isn't your thing, don't worry further on in the guide you will find a range of delicious cheap eats in Paris that deserve a Michelin-Star.
- While money can't buy happiness, it can buy cake and isn't that sort of the same thing? Jokes aside, Boulangerie Utopie (20 Rue Jean-Pierre Timbaud) in Paris have turned cakes and pastries into edible art. Visit to taste the most delicious croissant in Paris.
- While you might not be staying in a penthouse, you can still enjoy the same views. Visit rooftop bars in Paris, like the very affordable one one the last floor of Generator Paris - Khayma Rooftop Bar, to enjoy incredible sunset views for low prices. And if you want to continue enjoying libations, head over to The Crocodile (Address: 6 Rue Royer-Collard) for a dirt-cheap happy hour, lots of reasonably priced (and delicious) cocktails and cheap delicious snacks.

- Walking out of a salon or barber shop with a fresh cut makes most people feel rich. As the maxim goes, if you look good, you feel good. If you crave that freshly blow-dried or trimmed look, become a hair model for Toni&Guy Hairdressing Academy.. You'll receive a free cut/colour or wash. Of course, always agree on the look with your stylist.

Those are just some ideas for you to know that visiting Paris on a budget doesn't have to feel like sacrifice or con-striction. Now let's get into the nuts and bolts of Paris on the super cheap.

Things You Should Know Before You Visit Paris

Arrondissements

Arrondissements are the administrative districts of Paris. These districts are divided into twenty regions, each with its own mayor and arrondissement council. They are named after the landmarks they surround. These districts are numbered in a spiral, starting with the 1st Arrondissement at the Seine.

The 1st arrondissement is the tourist area. It is home to the Louvre, which is the world's largest art museum. It is also home to the Palais-Royal, an elegant palace. There are a number of interesting museums, shops, and monuments. The best way to explore the area is to visit in the early morning, before the crowds arrive.

INSIDER TIP: You must visit the Latin Quarter (5th arrondissement)

Located on the left bank of the Seine, the Latin Quarter in Paris is a famous historical district. A great place to explore, this district is brimming with museums and historical buildings.

The Latin Quarter was originally a bohemian enclave. Students used to meet in cafes and debate ideas; the Sorbonne and the College de France are located here.

The Latin Quarter is also home to the largest concentration of museums in Paris. The Museum of the Middle Ages is located in the magnificent Hotel de Cluny. Other historical sites in the area include the Roman bath house, which is the oldest preserved site in Paris.

The Pantheon is another prominent building in the Latin Quarter. This dome was originally a church, but later became a tomb for all the great people. In its history, the Pantheon has been the burial place for famous writers, artists, and musicians. Other notable tombs include Alexandre Dumas, Victor Hugo, and Marie Curie.

Restaurants in touristy places aren't usually the best

Generally speaking, restaurants in touristy places in Paris aren't usually the best. Oftentimes, they're bland and boring, and the food can be mediocre at best. Star the many cheap eats in the guide on Google Maps so you don't just wander in somewhere overpriced.

If in doubt, head to the 10th arrondissement. This is the epicenter of the left bank's buzziest culture hotspot, and you'll find some of the city's finest small restaurants.

Avoid expensive rooftops

Drinks at many rooftop bars in Paris average $25. It's not always easy to find a rooftop that's quiet enough to relax and cheap, The Holidays Inn is one such place. This roof top bar and restaurant is located in the heart of the Saint Michel district. It's not the prettiest, but it does have a nice view. You can enjoy a drink or two from 6EUR. The best thing about visiting a rooftop is that you get to see the city's best view without having to brave the crowds.

Avoid awkwardly misplaced lips and shuffle of heads

Parisians 'la bise' is a kiss on both cheeks.

Fines

The fine for dropping cigarette butts is currently EUR68.

Planning your trip

When to visit Paris

The first step in saving money on your Paris trip is timing.
If you are not tied to school holidays, the best time to visit is during the shoulder-season months of April or October, the weather is conducive to long hours of sightseeing and the summer crowds haven't yet arrived. The cheapest times to visit (prices drop 30% for accommodation then) are December, January, and February - it is cold and wet but still as beautiful. Don't despair if you are visiting during peak times there are innumerable hacks to save on accommodation in Paris which we will detail.

Visit Paris on your birthday

Visit Paris on your birthday you can get well over $250 of free entries, meals, cakes and more. All you need is a valid ID to claim your birthday gifts.

Here are the free entries:

The stars of Paris offer visitors a free cruise on their birthday (during the day). "accompanied by a free tasting for the person concerned, every day and for all departures on presentation of an identity document on their birthday. The cruises depart from the Eiffel Tower and cross historic Paris (Grand Palais, Place de la Concorde, the National Assembly, Musée d'Orsay, Louvre, Hôtel de Ville and Notre Dame)."

And here's where you can sample a free meal, birthday treat or heavy discount:

- Buffalo grill: cake offered to the table on your birthday

- Crocodile: free bottle of wine

- El rancho: 20 euros discount on your bill

- Memphis Coffee: 15 euro discount
- Starbucks: your favourite drink offered when you show your ID AND loyalty card.

What's on in Paris Month-by-month

January - La Grande Parade de Montmartre. Since 1993 thousands have flocked to Paris' 18th Arrondissment for this annual colourful parade.

February - Chinese New Year Celebrations Every year a huge parade marches its way through Paris' 'Quartier Chinois' to celebrate the coming of the New Year.

March - Banlieues Bleues Festival Paris' most important blues festival event in the Seine St Denis suburb.

May - Montmartre Vintage Car Rally.

June - Fête de la Musique - free concert all over Paris on the longest day of the year.

July - Bastille Day Commemorating the uprising that marked the beginning of the French Revolution.

August - Festival Rock en Seine The annual 2-day Festival Rock en Seine.

October - White Night in Paris One night every October many of Paris' libraries, museums and parks stay open all night.
December - New Year's Celebrations with spectacular fireworks.

Where to stay?

Ideally we'd all have a bath tub with a view to the Eiffel tower, but in a city of 2.2 million people it's a tough ask. The double-digit arrondissements (districts), with the exception of the 17th and 18th are the more affordable areas. Gare du Nord is a budget travellers area because of its close proximity to Eurostar, but some find it a bit dirty. I have stayed there four times, and never had any problems but if you are looking for a chic area to stay, the double-digit arrondissements are best, you can use the metro to get into the city easily.

St Christopher's Inn Canal
 is the best reviewed hostel in Paris and offers dorms from $20 a night. If you're travelling as a group, hotels are your best bang for your buck. Airbnbs are expensive in Paris due to high taxes.

If you want to experience Parisian nightlife book a hostel along Canal St. Martin. It's the young hipster capital of the city.

What Areas Are Dangerous in Paris?

Fortunately, most of the city is safe, but it's important to know where to avoid when you're booking accommodation.

Paris 19th is one area to avoid. The area is located in Jaures and Riquet Stalingrad, and is statistically home to the most crime in Paris.

Porte de la Chapelle and Marx Dormoy are also areas to avoid. These metro stations are known for being dodgy at night, and homeless people often hang around there.

Airbnb v Hotels

You can find a lot of cheap eats in Paris. Or do as the Parisians do: buy cheese and baguettes and dine on picnics in the park. You don't really need a kitchen to save money on food in Paris as there's a lot of delicious ready to eat food in the supermarkets. Plus Airbnbs in Paris average out at $157 a night. Hotels are actually cheaper and if a free-breakfast is included, better value.

The cheapest hotel deals are available when you 'blind book'. This means you don't know the name of the hotel before you book. But buy Googling the details you can normally find out the name of the hotel before you book. Use Last Minute Top Secret hotels and you can find a four star hotel from $80 a night in Paris! https://www.lastminute.com/hotels/france/paris/4-star-top-secret-hotel-in-paris

AVOID The weekend price hike in peak season

Hostel and hotel prices skyrocket during weekends in peak season. If you can get out of Paris for the weekend if you visit in the peak season you'll save $$$ on your accommodation. For example a dorm room at a popular Hostel costs $44 a night during the week. That price goes to $253 for Saturday's and Sundays.

Local Discount Accommodation

Aside from Booking and Airbnb you can find discount bed & breakfast, camping, couch-surfing and university residences accommodation on https://www.france-hotel-guide.com/en/cheap-hotels.php

Hack your Paris Accommodation

Your two biggest expenses when travelling to Paris are accommodation and food. This section is intended to help you cut these costs dramatically before and while you are in Paris.

Hostels are the cheapest accommodation in Paris but there are some creative workarounds to upgrade your stay on the cheap.

Use Time

There are two ways to use time. One is to book in advance. Three months will net you the best deal, especially if your visit coincides with an event. The other is to book on the day of your stay. This is a risky move, but if executed well, you can lay your head in a five-star hotel for a 2-star fee.

Before I travelled to Paris, I checked for big events using a simple google search 'What's on in Paris', there were no big events drawing travellers so I risked showing up with no accommodation booked (If there are big events on demand exceeds supply and you should avoid using this strategy) I started checking for discount rooms at 11 am using a private browser on booking.com.

Before I go into demand-based pricing, take a moment to think about your risk tolerance. By risk, I am not talking about personal safety. No amount of financial savings is worth risking that. What I am talking about is being inconvenienced. Do you deal well with last-minute changes? Can you roll with the punches or do you dislike it if something changes? Everyone is different and knowing yourself is the best way to plan a great trip. If you are someone that likes to have everything pre-planned using demand-based pricing to get cheap accommodation will not work for you.

Skip this section and go to blind-booking.

Demand-based pricing

Be they an Airbnb host or hotel manager; no one wants empty rooms. Most will do anything to make some revenue because they still have the same costs to cover whether the room is occupied or not. That's why you will find many hotels drastically slashing room rates for same-day bookings.

How to book five-star hotels for a two-star price

You will not be able to find these discounts when the demand exceeds the supply. So if you're visiting during the peak season, or during an event which has drawn many travellers don't try this.

On the day of your stay, visit booking.com (which offers better discounts than Kayak and agoda.com). Hotel Tonight individually checks for any last-minute bookings, but they take a big chunk of the action, so the better deals come from booking.com. The best results come from booking between 2 pm and 4 pm when the risk of losing any revenue with no occupancy is most pronounced, so algorithms supporting hotels slash prices. This is when you can find rates that are not within the "lowest publicly visible" rate. To avoid losing customers to other websites, or cheapening the image of their hotel most will only offer the super cheap rates during a two hour window from 2 pm to 4 pm. Two guests will pay 10x difference in price but it's absolutely vital to the hotel that neither knows it.

Takeaway: To get the lowest price book on the day of stay between 2 pm and 4 pm and extend your search radius to include further afield hotels with good transport connections.

Priceline Hack to get a Luxury Hotel on the Cheap

Priceline.com has been around since 1997 and is an incredible site for sourcing luxury Hotels on the cheap in Paris. If you've tried everything else and that's failed, priceline will deliver.

Priceline have a database of the lowest price a hotel will accept for a particular time and date. That amount changes depending on two factors:

1. Demand: More demand high prices.
2. Likelihood of lost revenue: if the room is still available at 3pm the same-day prices will plummet.

Obviously they don't want you to know the lowest price as they make more commission the higher the price you pay.

They offer two good deals to entice you to book with them in Paris. **And the good news is neither require last-minute booking (though the price will decrease the closer to the date you book).**

'Firstly, 'price-breakers'. You blind book from a choice of three highly rated hotels which they name. Pricebreakers, travelers are shown three similar, highly-rated hotels, listed under a single low price.' After you book they reveal the name of the hotel.

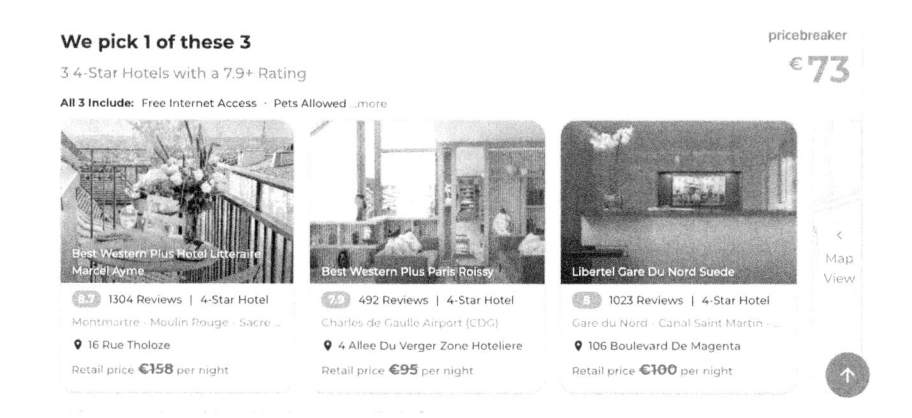

We pick 1 of these 3

3 4-Star Hotels with a 7.9+ Rating

All 3 Include: Free Internet Access · Pets Allowed ...more

Best Western Plus Hotel Litteraire Marcel Ayme
8.7 1304 Reviews | 4-Star Hotel
Montmartre - Moulin Rouge - Sacre ...
16 Rue Tholoze
Retail price €158 per night

Best Western Plus Paris Roissy
7.5 492 Reviews | 4-Star Hotel
Charles de Gaulle Airport (CDG)
4 Allee Du Verger Zone Hoteliere
Retail price €95 per night

Libertel Gare Du Nord Suede
8 1023 Reviews | 4-Star Hotel
Gare du Nord - Canal Saint Martin - ...
106 Boulevard De Magenta
Retail price €100 per night

Map View

Secondly, the 'express deals'. These are the last minute deals. You'll be able to see the name of the hotel before you book.

To find the right luxury hotel for you at a cheap price you should plug in the androissements you want to stay in, an acceptable rating (4 or 5 stars), and filter by the amenities you want.

How to trick travel Algorithms to get the lowest hotel price

Do not believe anyone who says changing your IP address to get cheaper hotels or flights does NOT work. If you don't believe us, download a Tor Network and search for flights and hotels to one destination using your current IP and then the tor network (a tor browser hits your IP address from algorithms. It is commonly used by hackers). You will receive different prices.

The price you see is a decision made by an algorithm that adjusts prices using data points such as past bookings, remaining capacity, average demand and the probability of selling the room or flight later at a higher price. If knows you've searched for the area before it will keep the prices high. To circumvent this, you can either use a different IP address from a cafe or airport or data from an international sim. I use a sim from Three, which provides free data in many countries around the world. When you search from a new IP address, most of the time, and particularly near booking you will get a lower price. Sometimes if your sim comes from a 'rich' country, say the UK or USA, you will see higher rates as the algorithm has learnt people from these countries pay more. The solution is to book from a local wifi connection - but a different one from the one you originally searched from.

How to get last-minute discounts on owner rented properties

In addition to Airbnb, you can also find owner rented rooms and apartments on www.vrbo.com or HomeAway or a host of others. Nearly all owners renting accommodation will happily give renters a "last-minute" discount to avoid the space sitting empty, not earning a dime.

Go to Airbnb or another platform and put in today's date. Once you've found something you like start the negotiating by asking for a 25% reduction. A sample message to an Airbnb host might read:

Dear HOST NAME,

I love your apartment. It looks perfect for me. Unfortunately, I'm on a very tight budget. I hope you won't be offended, but I wanted to ask if you would be amenable to offering me a 25% discount for tonight, tomorrow and the following day? I see that you aren't booked. I can assure you, I will leave your place exactly the way I found it. I will put bed linen in the washer and ensure everything is clean for the next guest. I would be delighted to bring you a bottle of wine to thank you for any discount that you could offer.

If this sounds okay, please send me a custom offer, and I will book straight away.

YOUR NAME.

In my experience, a polite, genuine message like this, that proposes reciprocity will be successful 80% of the time. Don't ask for more than 25% off, this person still has to pay the bills and will probably say no as your stay will cost them more in bills than they make. Plus starting higher, can offend the owner and do you want to stay somewhere, where you have offended the host?

In Practice

To use either of these methods, you must travel light. Less stuff means greater mobility, everything is faster and you don't have to check-in or store luggage. If you have a lot of luggage, you're going to have fewer of these opportunities to save on accommodation. Plus travelling light benefits the planet - you're buying, consuming, and transporting less stuff.

Blind-booking

If your risk tolerance does not allow for last-minute booking, you can use blind-booking. Many hotels not wanting to cheapen their brand with known low-prices, choose to operate a blind booking policy. This is where you book without knowing the name of the hotel you're going to stay in until you've made the payment. This is also sometimes used as a marketing strategy where the hotel is seeking to recover from past issues. I've stayed in plenty of blind book hotels. As long as you choose 4 or 5 star hotels, you will find them to be clean, comfortable and safe. priceline.com, Hot Rate® Hotels and Top Secret Hotels (operated by last-minute.com) offer the best deals.

Hotels.com Loyalty Program

This is currently the best hotel loyalty program with hotels in Paris. The basic premise is you collect 10 nights and get 1 free. hotels.com price match, so if booking.com has a cheaper price you can get hotel.com, to match. If you intend to travel more than ten nights in a year, its a great choice to get the 11th free.

Don't let time use you

Rigidity will cost you money. You pay the price you're willing to pay, not the amount it requires a hotel to deliver. Therefore if you're in town for a big event, saving money on accommodation is nearly impossible so in such cases book three months ahead.

The best price performance location in Paris

A room putting Paris's attractions, restaurants, and nightlife within walking distance will save you time on transport. However restaurants and bars do get much cheaper the further you go from famous tourist attractions. You will also get a better idea of the day to day life of a local if you stay in a neighbourhood like the 20th arrondissement. It depends on the Paris you want to experience. For the tourist experience stay in the centre either in a last-minute hotel or Airbnb. For a taste of local life the leafy district of 20th arrondissement is the best you will find. Chopin, Edith Piaf,

Proust and Oscar Wilde all lived there at one time.
<u>Hôtel Tamaris</u> is a luxurious hotel with rooms from $40 a night in the 20th arrondissement.

INSIDER MONEY SAVING TIP

You can stay for free in a shop frequented by Hemingway and James Joyce. Shakespesre & Co. has hosted over 30,000 "Tumbleweeds" who stay for free in exchange for helping out in the shop and reading and writing. Call or email if you're interested in staying with them for free. Shakespeare & Company and Abbey Bookshop also host free book reading and literary events throughout the year - worth checking out while you're in town.

How to be a green tourist in Paris

Paris like other major urban metropolis battles with air pollution; it's important as responsible tourists that we help not hinder Paris. There is a bizarre misconception that you have to spend money to travel in an eco-friendly way. This like, all marketing myths was concocted and hyped by companies seeking to make money off of you. In my experience, anything with eco in front of their names e.g Eco-tours will be triple the cost of the regular tour. Don't get me wrong sometimes its best to take these tours if you're visiting endangered areas, but normally such places have extensive legislation that everyone, including the eco and non-eco tour operators must comply with. The vast majority of ways you can travel eco-friendly are free and even save you money:

- Avoid Bottled Water - get a good water bottle and re-fill. The water in Paris is safe to drink.

- Thrift shop but check the labels and don't buy poly-ester clothes - overtime plastic is released into the ocean when we wash polyester.

- Don't put it in a plastic bag, bring a cotton tote with you when you venture out. If you pick up a local one from a Parians supermarket, this will also disguise you as a local.

- Pack Light - this is one of the best ways to save money. If you find a 5-star hotel for tonight for $10, and you're at an Airbnb or hostel, you can easily pack and upgrade hassle-free. A light pack equals freedom and it means less to wash.

- Travel around Paris on Bikes or e-Scooters or use Public Transportation.

- Car Pool with services like bla bla car or Uber/Lyft share.

- Walk, this is the best way to get to know Paris. You never know what's around the corner.

- Travel Overland - this isn't always viable especially if you only have limited time off work, but where possible avoid flying and if you have to compensate by offsetting or keeping the rest of your trip carbon-neutral by doing all of the above.

Saving money on Paris Food

Use 'Too Good To Go'

Paris offers plenty of food bargains; if you know where to look. Thankfully the app 'Too Good to Go' is turning visitors into locals by showing them exactly where to find the tastiest deals and simultaneously rescue food that would otherwise be wasted. In Paris you can pick up a $15 buy of baked goods, groceries, breakfast, brunch, lunch or dinner boxes for $2.99. You'll find lots of fish and meat dishes on offer in Paris, which would normally be expensive.

How it works?
You pay for a magic bag (essentially a bag of what the restaurant or bakery has leftover) on the app and simply pick it up from the bakery or restaurant during the time they've selected. You can find extremely cheap breakfast, lunch, dinner and even groceries this way. Simply download the app and press 'my current location' to find the deals near you in Paris.
https://toogoodtogo.org/en
.What's not to love about restaurant quality delicious food thats a quarter of the normal price and helping to drive down food waste?

An oft-quoted parable is 'There is no such thing as cheap food. Either you pay at the cash registry or the doctor's office'. This dismisses the fact that good nutrition is a choice; we all make every-time we eat. Cheap eats are not confined to hotdogs and kebabs. The great thing about using Too Good To Go is you can eat nutritious food cheaply: fruits, vegetables, fish and nut dishes are a fraction of their supermarket cost.

Japan has the longest life expectancy in the world. A national study by the Japanese Ministry of Internal Affairs and Communications revealed that between January and May 2019, a household of two spent on average ¥65,994 a month, that's $10 per person per day on food. You truly don't need to spend a lot to eat nutritious food. That's a marketing gimmick hawkers of overpriced muesli bars want you to believe.

Check out this local Facebook group (https://www.facebook.com/groups/106098493560800/about/) where people share pictures of the food they picked up from restaurants and supermarkets in Paris. It's a great way to see what's on offer and find food you'll love.

Breakfast

If you stay somewhere with a free breakfast, eat smart. Don't eat sugary cereals or white flour rich pastries if you don't want to be hungry an hour later. Before leaving your hotel or checking out, find some fresh fruit, water, and granola in the fitness centre or coffee in the lobby or business centre. If your hotel doesn't have free breakfast, don't take it. You can always eat cheaper outside. Mich'sandwiches (not a typo, the name of the cafe) has the best cheap breakfast we found. Here you can pick up crepes for less than $2.

Visit supermarkets at discount times.

You can get a 50 per cent discount around 5 pm at the Carrefour supermarkets on fresh produce. The cheaper the supermarket, the less discounts you will find, so check Carrefour's at 5 pm instead of discount supermarkets. Some items are also marked down due to sell-by date after the lunchtime rush so its also worth to check in around 3 pm. Don't buy anything at Monoprix. It is so expensive. Lidl is so much cheaper.

Do grocery shopping online

Apps like Getir give you 15% off your first grocery shop in Paris.

Use delivery services on the cheap
Take advantage of local offers on food delivery services. Most platforms including Uber Eats and Foodora offer $10 off the first order in Paris.

SNAPSHOT: How to enjoy a $5,000 trip to Paris for $500

(full breakdown at the end of the guide)

Stay	Blind book a hotel or use Priceline pricebreakers to get a 4 or 5 star hotel for under $80 a night in the low season.
Eat	You don't need to spend a fortune in Paris to eat memorable food. Average meal cost: $6 - $12. Use Too Good To Go for a couple of restaurant dinners to save $200+
Move	Metro with Navigo card
See	Muséums, monuments, shops,p parks, art and music $70
Experience	Michelin-starred restaurants and rooftop bars
Total	US$500

Unique bargains we love in Paris

As you know Paris has the reputation of being among the most luxurious and expensive cities in the world. Fortunately, some of the best things in life are free (or almost free). Eat street food like crepes and from bakeries or supermarkets. Buy an eclair from La Galette des Moulins in Montmartre (cheaper and better eclairs than the fancy well known ones) and after eating the eclair, the first thing you should do when you arrive is check http://www.freeinparis.com/free-paris/ to see what free events are on.

Avoid staying close to the city centre/ Eiffel Tower. Everything (like accommodation and dining) is more expensive the closer you get.

Paris has some of the best flea markets; there are bargains to be found if you don't mind sifting through endless clothing rails. The St-Ouen Flea Market (Porte de Clignacourt, 18th Arrondisse- ment) is the largest of its kind in the world and while it markets itself as an antique market, you will find many amazing second hand designer pieces. Porte de Vanves Flea Market (Blvd. Lefebvre, 14th Arrondissement.) is also great for clothes. Visit rue Cler - a cool little market street with an amazing and cheap cheese shop: La Fromagerie. Even the most reluctant bargain hunter can be successful in Paris. There's so much to see and do cheaply that you will be planning your second visit.

It's also a good idea to visit the tourism office. They may offer discounts on tours and attractions.

Take your student card

Paris offers hundreds of student discounts. If you're studying buy an ISIC card - International Student Identity Card. It's a great investment because its valid in 133 countries and covers 150,000 discounts including many hundreds in Paris.

Senior discounts

Nearly every major museum, attraction and local transport offers reduced fares for seniors age 65.

How to use this book

Google and TripAdvisor are your on-the-go guides while traveling, a travel guide adds the most value during the planning phase, and if you're without Wi-Fi. Always download the google map for your destination - having an offline map will make using this guide much more comfortable. For ease of use, we've set the book out the way you travel, booking your flights, arriving, how to get around, then on to the money-saving tips. The tips we ordered according to when you need to know the tip to save money, so free tours and combination tickets feature first. We prioritized the rest of the tips by how much money you can save and then by how likely it was that you could find the tip with a google search. Meaning those we think you could find alone are nearer the bottom. I hope you find this layout useful. If you have any ideas about making Super Cheap Insider Guides easier to use, please email me philgattang@gmail.com

A quick note on How We Source Super Cheap Tips
We focus entirely on finding the best bargains. We give each of our collaborators $2,000 to hunt down never-before-seen deals. The type you either only know if you're local or by on the ground research. We spend zero on marketing and a little on designing an excellent cover. We do this yearly, which means we just keep finding more amazing ways for you to have the same experience for less.

Now let's get started with juicing the most pleasure from your trip to Paris with the least possible money!

OUR SUPER CHEAP TIPS...

How to Find Super Cheap Flights to Paris

Luck is just an illusion. Anyone can find incredible flight deals. If you can be flexible you can save huge amounts of money. In fact, the biggest tip I can give you for finding incredible flight deals is simple: find a flexible job. Don't despair if you can't do that theres still a lot you can do. The following pages detail the exact method I use to consistently find cheap flights to Paris.

Book your flight to Paris on a Tuesday or Wednesday

Tuesdays and Wednesdays are the cheapest days of the week to fly. You can take a flight to Paris on a Tuesday or Wednesday for less than half the price you'd pay on a Thursday Friday, Saturday, Sunday or Monday.

Cheapest route to Paris from America

The cheapest way to Paris is from NYC - booking one-way tickets reduces the cost. Level is the cheapest operator offering tickets consistently from $113.

Start with Google Flights (but never book with them)

I conduct upwards of 50 flight searches a day for readers. I use google flights first when looking for flights. I put specific departure but broad destination (e.g Europe) and usually find amazing deals.

The great thing about Google Flights is you can search by class. You can pick a specific destination and it will tell you which time is cheapest in which class. Or you can put in dates and you can see which area is cheapest to travel to.

But be aware Google flights does not show the cheapest prices among the flight search engines but it does offer several advantages

1. You can see the cheapest dates for the next 8 weeks. Other search engines will blackout over 70% of the prices.
2. You can put in multiple airports to fly from. Just use a common to separate in the from input.
3. If you're flexible on where you're going Google flights can show you the cheapest destinations.
4. You can set-up price tracking, where Google will email you when prices rise or decline.

Once you have established the cheapest dates to fly go over to skyscanner.net and put those dates in. You will find sky scanner offers the cheapest flights.

Get Alerts when Prices to Paris are Lowest

Google also has a nice feature which allows you to set up an alert to email you when prices to your destination are at their lowest. So if you don't have fixed dates this feature can save you a fortune.

Baggage add-ons

It may be cheaper and more convenient to send your luggage separately with a service like sendmybag.com Often the luggage sending fee is cheaper than what the airlines charge to check baggage. Visit Lugless.-com or luggagefree.com in addition to sendmybag.com for a quotation.

Loading times

Anyone who has attempted to find a cheap flight will know the pain of excruciating long loading times. If you encounter this issue use google flights to find the cheapest dates and then go to skyscanner.net for the lowest price.

Always try to book direct with the airline

Once you have found the cheapest flight go direct to the airlines booking page. This is advantageous in the current cancellation climate, because if you need to change your flights or arrange a refund, its much easier to do so, than via a third party booking agent.

That said, sometimes the third party bookers offer cheaper deals than the airline, so you need to make the decision based on how likely you think it is that disruption will impede you making those flights.

More flight tricks and tips

www.secretflying.com/usa-deals offers a range of deals from the USA and other countries. For example you can pick-up a round trip flight non-stop from from the east coast to johannes-burg for $350 return on this site

Scott's cheap flights, you can select your home airport and get emails on deals but you pay for an annual subscription. A free workaround is to download Hopper and set search alerts for trips/ price drops.

Premium service of Scott's cheap flights.
They sometime have discounted business and first class but in my experience they are few and far between.

JGOOT.com has 5 times as many choices as Scott's cheap flights.

kiwi.com allows you to be able to do radius searches so you can find cheaper flights to general areas.

Finding Error Fares
Travel Pirates (www.travelpirates.com) is a gold-mine for finding error deals. Subscribe to their newsletter. I recently found a reader an airfare from Montreal-Brazil for a $200 round trip (mistake fare!). Of course these error fares are always certain dates, but if you can be flexible you can save a lot of money.

Things you can do that might reduce the fare to Paris:--
- Use a VPN (if the booker knows you booked one-way, the return fare will go up)
- Buy your ticket in a different currency

How to Find CHEAP FIRST-CLASS Flights to Paris

Upgrade at the airport
Airlines are extremely reluctant to advertise price drops in first or business class tickets so the best way to secure them is actually at the airport when airlines have no choice but to decrease prices dramatically because otherwise they lose money. Ask about up-grading to business or first-class when you check-in. If you check-in online look around the airport for your airlines branded bidding system. For example KLM at Amsterdam have terminals where you can bid on upgrades.

Use Air-miles

When it comes to accruing air-miles for American citizens **Chase Sapphire Reserve card** ranks top. If you put everything on there and pay it off immediately you will end up getting free flights all the time, aside from taxes.

Get 2-3 chase cards with sign up bonuses, you'll have 200k points in no time and can book with points on multiple airlines when transferring your points to them.

Please note, this is only applicable to those living in the USA. In the Bonus Section we have detailed the best air-mile credit cards for those living in the UK, Canada, Germany, Austria, Spain and Australia.

How many miles does it take to fly first class?
For example first class from NYC to Paris costs 80,000 miles.

Arriving

From the airport

The cheapest way from the Charles De Gaulle airport is with the ARATP bus 350 (€6; 70 minutes; every 30 minutes, 5.30am to 11pm). The bus Links the airport with Gare de l'Est in northern Paris.

If you fly into Orly airport, the bus costs €12 to the centre of Paris. It takes about 35 minutes. The only other option is Uber which costs 30 euros.

INSIDER MONEY SAVING TIP
Cheap Eurostar. Booking three months in advance on eurostar.com can net you tickets for $35 from London to Paris.

Need a place to store luggage?
Use stasher.com to find a convenient place to store your luggage cheaply. It provides much cheaper options than airport and train station lockers in Paris.

Getting around

The official arrondissements (districts) of Paris number 20 but there are also a number of informal districts in the city. Each with its own character. If you want to cross Paris from north to south, it would take you only two hours walking. Paris is a city that rewards those who explore it by foot. Pack good walking shoes and walk.

Bike

Paris is a lovely city to cycle. Like a growing number of cities around the world, Paris has an established bike-sharing program. It is called velib. You pay a fee of 3 EUR for a day-ticket or 15 Euro for a week ticket. You can use any bicycle from the velib network.

E-scooters

Paris has e-scooters (Lime, Bird and Dott are the main providers) but you can only ride them on roads and bike lanes, if you're caught on the footpath it's an on-the-spot fine of €130.

The metro

The Paris Metro has over 300 Paris stations on 16 lines covering the 10x10km area of central Paris. It is one of the most well-connected cities in the world. It costs 1.90€ for a single ticket to ride the metro but its cheaper to buy 10 tickets, a carnet ["car-nay"] for 14.90€ but a Navigo pass is better value.

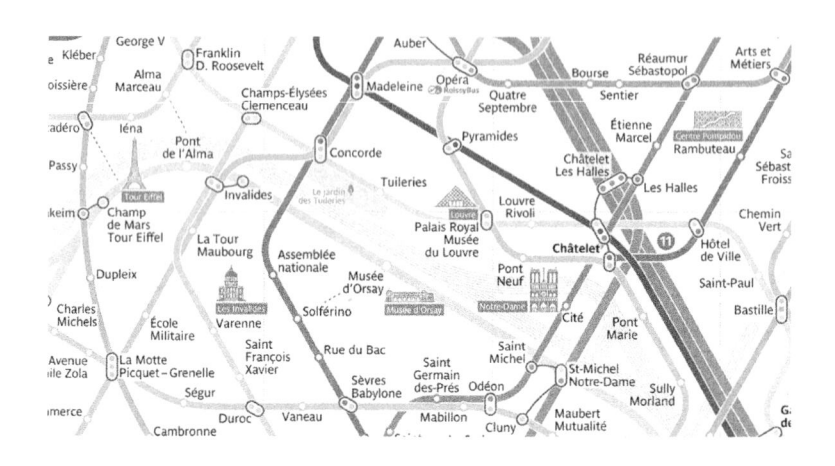

The Paris Métro

Get a Navigo decouverte pass

With a Navigo pass, you may travel on every Metro line,
all RER (Regional Express Network) and Transilien train lines, all bus lines (except Orlybus and Roissybus) and all Tram lines in the Paris region, as well as the Montmartre Funicular
From 19.85€ per week. Scan the QR code below to register for one - its free.

Insider tips for travelling on the Paris Metro

1. Avoid rush hour (4pm - 6pm).

2. Keep your ticket at all times, random inspections are common and you will be fined if you can't show a valid ticket.

3. If you're travelling alone, avoid these stations at night: Châtelet–Les Halles and its corridors; Château Rouge in Montmartre; Gare du Nord; Strasbourg St-

Denis; Réaumur Sébastopol; and Montparnasse Bienvenüe.

4. Beware of your surrounding and keep an eye on your belongings.

5. Disguise yourself as a local by buying a local branded reusable supermarket bag.

INSIDER CULTURAL INSIGHT

If you want to see Paris in a totally unique way make sure your trip includes a Friday night. Every Friday night since 1993 at 10pm roller bladers meet at Place Raoul-Dautry in Montparnasse for a three-hour, 30km (19-mile) tour around Paris. It's totally free to join you just need a pair of roller blades. For more information visit www.pari-roller.com

Orientate yourself with a free tour

Forget exploring Paris by wandering around aimlessly. Always start with a free organised tour. Nothing compares to local advice, especially when travelling on a budget. We gleamed many of our super cheap tips from local guides and locals in general, so start with a organised tour to get your bearings and ask for their recommendations for the best cheap eats, the best bargains, the best markets, the best place for a particular street eat. Perhaps some of it will be repeated from this guide, but it can't hurt to ask, especially if you have specific needs or questions. At the end you should leave an appropriate tip (usually around $5), but nobody bats an eye lid if you are unable or unwilling to do so, tell them you will leave a good review and always give them a little gift from home - I always carry small Vienna fridge magnets and I always tip the $5, but it is totally up to you.

I pre-booked the Paris Greeters tour (www.greeters.Paris) where you get to see Paris through local eyes for these two- to three-hours.
https://greeters.paris/en/meet-a-greeter/
 (you must book at least four weeks in advance)

You can also do over 12 different free walking tours depending on what you're interested in: https://freetoursbyfoot.com/paris-tours/ has a comprehensive list.

If you have more time consider Geocaching.
This is where you hunt for hide-and-seek containers. You need a mobile device to follow the GPS clues in Paris. A typical cache is a small, waterproof container with a logbook where you can leave a message or see various trinkets left by other cache hunters. Build your own treasure hunt by discovering geocaches in Paris.
www.geocaching.com

TOP TIP
If the centre of Paris gets too much for you, retreat to Galerie Vero-Dodat. It is a covered passage that runs between the Palais-Royal and Les Halles. It has become one of Paris's secret spots.

The passage is a great place to find a table to relax and enjoy a meal. There are numerous restaurants here, including the Restaurant Vero-Dodat, which has been serving traditional French food for over twenty years.

.

Consider Paris's combination PASSES

Attraction aficionados can save money with combo passes in Paris. There are a couple of different options:

1. the Paris Pass

2. Paris Passlib'

3. the Paris Museum pass

Paris Pass

It works out cheaper to just pay for the attractions al a carte, or by buying tickets on groupons, buy discounted tickets etc than to buy the Paris Pass. In my opinion it is just a collection of existing passes and tickets put into an envelope, and sold for far more than the cost of the individual components.

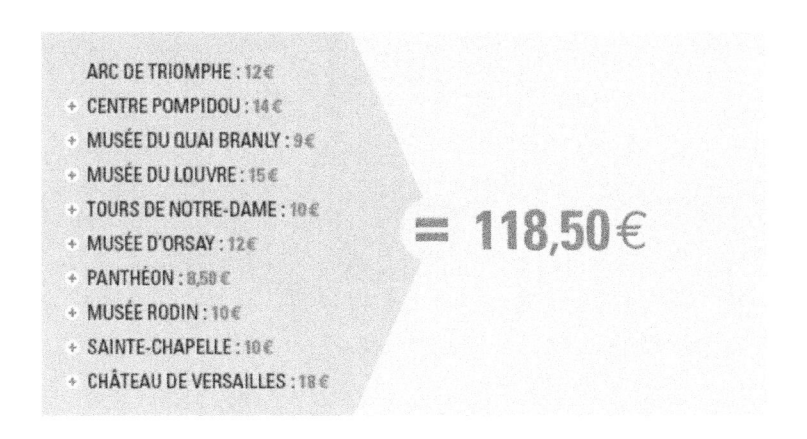

Paris Passlib'

€109 for two days of unlimited public transport in zones 1 to 3, a Paris Museum Pass, a one-hour boat cruise, and a one-day bus tour with L'Open Tour.

The Paris Museum Pass

Offers the best bang for your buck. Costing €48 for two days with potential savings of €70 if you visit all the included attractions - see parismuesumpass.com plus you can bypass long ticket queues.

Note: There are long lines for most attractions even with the Passes. And at several attractions it was faster in the pre-paid or paid lines. Go early to avoid queuing. And be mindful of your bags while queuing at tourist attractions.

Can you already get in for free?
For students and seniors with valid ID; children and students who are EU citizens under 26 admission to most museums is free in Paris.

INSIDER HISTORICAL INSIGHT
Celtic people first settled Paris giving it the name Parisii. The name Parisii was later shortened in 508 A.D. to Paris.

Visit these astonishing **<u>FREE</u>** Museums

Paris is home to 130 museums. Whether you are looking for a museum that has a focus on history, science, or art, Paris has a large variety of museums to choose from. To make sure everybody has access to culture many of Paris's top museums can be accessed for free at particular times and ALL are worth your time. Here are the best of the crop:

The following museums are **<u>Always</u>** free to visit

- Visit the permanent collections of Paris' *musées municipaux* (www.Paris.fr/musees) for free. These 14 municipal museums are full of treasures relatively unexplored by visitors to Paris.

- Pavillon de l'Arsenal - The Center for architecture and urbanism, a center for urban planning and museum located in the 4th arrondissement.

- Musée du Parfum - Paris' perfume museums with free guided tours. Come here to learn about the history, compositions of different perfumes and techniques of applying for free. Visit <u>https://musee-parfum-paris.fragonard.com/</u> for times of the free tour.

The following museums are **Free on the first Sunday of the month**. <u>Where Months are mentioned this is the time frame they are free on the first Sunday of the month.</u>

- Arc de Triomphe - This eponymous monument honours those who fought and died for France in the French Revolutionary and Napoleonic Wars. You can visit the ground level of the arch for free. Take the underpass to access the arch. Never attempt to cross the dangerous roundabout from the Champs Elysées! To access the top, you can climb 284 steps, or take an elevator to the mid-level and climb 64 stairs to the top. You can go to the top for free during November to March on the first Sunday of the month.

- Basilique de St-Denis Free November to March. This large medieval abbey church in the north of Paris is of singular importance historically and architecturally as it was completed in 1144.

- Château de Versailles Free November to March. Attracting millions of visitors annually, Versailles was the principal royal residence of France from 1682, under Louis XIV, until the French Revolution in 1789.

- Cité de l'Architecture et du Patrimoine - museum of architecture and monumental sculpture located in the Palais de Chaillot

- Conciergerie - Free November to March - located on the west of the Île de la Cité, formerly a prison but presently used mostly for law courts. It was part of the former royal palace, the Palais de la Cité.

- Musée des Arts et Métiers is an interesting industrial design museum that houses the collection of the Conservatoire national des arts et métiers, which was founded in 1794. Its free every Thursday from 6pm.

- Musée des Impressionnismes in Giverny - focused on the history of Impressionism. You can visit for free on the first Sunday of every month.

- Musée d'Orsay - Paris' most popular museum housed in the former Gare d'Orsay, a Beaux-Arts railway station built between 1898 and 1900. The museum holds mainly French art dating from 1848 to 1914. You can visit for free on the first Sunday of every month.

- Musée du Louvre - Free October to March.

- Musée Guimet des Arts Asiatiques - art museum located in the 16th arrondissement.

- Musée National d'Art Moderne Within the Centre Pompidou

- Musée National du Moyen Âge Aka Musée de Cluny

- Musée National Eugène Delacroix - art museum dedicated to painter Eugène Delacroix and located in the 6th arrondissement

- Musée National Gustave Moreau - art museum dedicated to Symbolist painter Gustave Moreau.

- Musée National Picasso - dedicated to the work of the Spanish artist Pablo Picasso

- Musée Rodin - free October to March. This museum is dedicated to the works of the French sculptor Auguste Rodin. The museum was opened in 1919 and is located in a mansion called Hotel Biron. Rodin donated many of his works, as well as his library, to the city of Paris.

- Panthéon free November to March.

- Musée de la Chasse et de la Nature - Exhibits focus on the relationships between humans and the natural environment through the traditions and practices of hunting.

- Musée de l'Histoire de l'Immigration - museum of immigration history located in the 12th arrondissement.

- Musée de l'Orangerie - art gallery of impressionist and post-impressionist paintings located in the west corner of the Tuileries Gardens next to the Place de la Concorde.

- Crypte Arhcéologique de Notre Dame is free every Sunday morning between 10am-1pm (but due to the recent fire is closed until 2024)

- Cognacq-jay musée: A small museum dedicated to the art and design of the old regime, and particularly the 18th century, housed in an old apartment,

BEWARE: Be mindful of your belongings in the Queues. They snake around and the huddle presents a great opportunity for pickpockets. Don't keep anything in your back pockets and keep your bags zipped and where you can see them.

INSIDER INSIGHT
You'd be in the Louvre 35 days straight to spend 30 seconds at each artwork housed there!

Visit Carnavalet Museum

Located in the city center, Carnavalet Museum is an art and history museum that offers a comprehensive look at Paris's history. Its collections include archaeological remains of Paris from the ancient era, Roman relics, and Belle Epoque mementos. It is the city's oldest museum.

In addition to the permanent collections, Carnavalet Museum organizes two large temporary exhibitions each year. The museum also has a bookshop, a museum store, and lectures and workshops.

Carnavalet Museum features the writing room of world-famous writer Marcel Proust. It also displays mementos of Napoleon Bonaparte and the French royal family.

The Carnavalet Museum has an impressive museum garden, decorated with sculptures representing the seasons. The courtyard also has an ancient arch decorated with bas-reliefs. It is free to enter and is open seven days a week, except Mondays. The museum's programs include a series of free lectures, workshops, and concerts. https://www.carnavalet.paris.fr/

Visit Musee de la Vie Romantique

Located in the 9th arrondissement, the Musee de la Vie Romantique, or the "Museum of Romantics," is one of the most romantic secret spots in Paris. It's located in a charming house that once belonged to a Dutch painter, Ary Scheffer.

This charming house is now a museum dedicated to the life and works of the Romantic era in France. It has two studios, a courtyard, a greenhouse, and a tearoom. The museum is free and open to the public, except on Mondays.

The Romanticism Museum aims to recreate the era of Romantic art, literature, and music. It's located in the Pigalle neighborhood. The museum includes paintings, sculptures, and other artifacts from the time. https://museevieromantique.paris.fr/fr

Visit a Queue Free Louvre

Founded in 1793, the Louvre Museum is located inside the Louvre Palace. It is the world's largest museum. It features over half a million works of art from around the world. It's famed for being home to Leonardo da Vinci's 1503 'Mona Lisa' the Louvre is a must-see but you don't need to queue for hours to enter.

WHERE TO ENTER
The Louvre is divided into three wings over four floors. The main entrance and ticket windows are covered by the glass pyramid designed IM Pei. Enter the Louvre complex via the underground shopping centre Carrousel du Louvre - 99 rue de Rivoli to avoid the queues and pickpockets who lurk around them.

The cheapest way to visit is with The Paris Museum Pass. Otherwise tickets cost €17 for adults.

NEED TO KNOW
- The Louvre Museum is divided into eight thematic departments. The main exhibits include Greek and Roman works from the Greek and Roman Empires, ancient Egyptian relics, and paintings from the 13th to 20th century.

- It costs €5 to rent an audio guide and or you can find free apps with similar content on app stores.
- The museum has a bookshop that features France's largest collection of art history books. It also carries guidebooks in various languages
- The Louvre is free always if you're under 26 and from the EU.

History of the Louvre

Originally built as a fortress in the 12th century, the Louvre became the residence of the French royal family from the 14th century until the French Revolution. After the Revolution, the Louvre became a museum.

The first art works to be displayed at the Louvre were works by the royal painters: Coypel, Mignard and Le Brun. These paintings were hung from floor to ceiling, with no labels to indicate who the artist was.

King Charles IX began building the Petite Galerie in 1566. It was designed to be a long building along the Seine River. The gallery was intended to connect the Louvre to the Tuileries Palace.

In the 17th century, the French monarchs began building new additions to their residence at the Louvre. The Colonnade was designed by a committee in 1667, with a monumental facade featuring a peristyle of double columns. The Pavillon de l'Horloge was built between the old and new buildings.

During the reign of Louis XVIII, the collection of art at the Louvre increased significantly. Some of the finest works of the Musee des Monuments Francais were transferred to the Louvre.
A few works from the sixteenth century are still part of the Louvre collection today. These include the Wedding at Cana and The Virgin and Child with St. Anne.

Climb the Eiffel Tower

The Eiffel tower is a defining symbol of Paris. The Eiffel Tower, La Tour Eiffel in French, was the main exhibit of the World's Fair of 1889. It was constructed to commemorate the centennial of the French Revolution and to demonstrate France's industrial prowess to the world. It was the world's tallest building when it was built in 1889. It was supposed to be a temporary structure, but is still here 130 years later. The views from the different observation decks are breathtaking. It is open daily from 9.30am-11.45pm admission €16.60 (second floor).

WHAT TO KNOW BEFORE YOU GO

- If you don't want to pay to go up the Eiffel Tower. Go to Quai Branly museum rooftop restaurant where you can get an incredible view of the Eiffel Tower for free.
- During the height of the tourist season, the Eiffel Tower can be packed to the gills. This means that you may need to be patient as you navigate your way through the ticket lines and elevator lines.
- Also, be aware that the tower is windier than you'd expect.
- The cheapest way to visit the Eiffel Tower is to purchase a ticket online. You can do so up to 60 days in advance of your visit.

- The tower has three levels: the first, the second, and the summit. The first floor is the largest of the three and offers unparalleled views of Paris. It also includes a museum and the historic spiral staircase. It has a gift shop and an interactive play area for kids.
- The second floor of the Eiffel Tower is home to the Jules Verne restaurant, which holds several Michelin stars. This is also where you can find the macaroon bar and the large observation deck. The first floor is home to the 58 Tour Eiffel restaurant, which has a lunch menu that starts at 47 euros.

History of the Eiffel Tower

In 1878, the firm Eiffel designed several buildings for the Paris World's Fair. The Eiffel Tower was designed by Maurice Koechlin and Emile Nouguier. Koechlin was the chief engineer for Eiffel's engineering company. Nouguier was a lesser known civil engineer. The Eiffel Tower was completed on March 31, 1889.

Some of the most prominent artists of the time were part of a campaign against the tower's construction. A group called the 'Committee of 300' formed to oppose the project. It consisted of notable figures in the arts and architecture such as Guy de Maupassant and Alfred Sisley.

The tower was also used for scientific experiments:

- It was meant to serve as a strategic observation post and optical telegraph communication post. Two million visitors came to the fair to view the tower.
- A radio transmitter on the tower blocked German communications in 1914.
- The tower also served as a beacon for Charles Lindbergh when he landed in Paris in 1927.
- The Eiffel Tower had its own laboratory on the top floor. The laboratory was used to study meteorology, aerodynamics, physiology, and astronomy. Scientists also tested Foucault's Pendulum.
- The tower was also used by the French military during World War I to intercept enemy messages.

- In the 1950s, the tower was installed with a radio transmitter that transmitted satellite signals.

Its height is approximately 324 meters. It is made of 7,300 tons of iron. The metal on the tower could expand and contract over time, which could weaken the structure. This is why the Eiffel Tower was painted in three shades to prevent rusting. The lights on the tower are considered an artwork, and are protected under EU copyright law. There are 20,000 lights on the tower.

During World War II,Hitler wanted to hang the German Reich flag from the top of the tower. However, the military commander in charge did not follow through with Hitler's orders. Instead, the lift cables were cut before the German flag could be hung.

In the 1960s, the tower was supposed to be moved to Canada for the Universal Exhibition, but Charles de Gaulle made a secret agreement with the mayor of Montreal to keep the tower in Paris.

Visit Versailles Palace on the cheap

Versailles is Louis XIV's gilded palace. It's prolific game attracted France's Kings and eventually lead to its construction. It is an immense, 18th-century palace with gilded apartments, chandelier lined Hall of Mirrors & fountain show. The site is surrounded by beautiful gardens that are decorated with sculptures and water features. The gardens have 600 fountains and 372 statues. The grounds of Versailles are the largest in the world. The gardens are so large that they are able to accommodate over 5,000 visitors at once!

The cheapest and easiest way to get to Versailles is by Paris RER train costing 3.65€.

NOTE: There are two main entrances to the Palace of Versailles. Gate A is for on-site ticket buyers, and Gate B is for skip the line ticket holders. There is a long queue at Gate A, and it can take up to 60 minutes to get in.

Over five million people visit Versailles annually. Follow these three tips for the most enjoyable experience:

1. Arrive early morning and avoid Tuesday, Saturday and Sundays - the busiest days.

2. Pre-purchase tickets on the château's website www.chateauversailles.fr to avoid **LONG** queues via gate B.
3. Download the free app from the website to give you a free audio guide of Versailles https://en.chateauver-sailles.fr/discover/resources/palace-versailles-appli-cation The palace is not only a stunning monument, but it is also the site of political significance and many famous personalities which the guide takes you through.

The History of Versailles

The Palace of Versailles was initially built as a hunting lodge for King Louis XIII. It was later enlarged into a royal residence by Louis XIV in the 1660s. During the construction of the Palace, thousands of workers were involved. These workers were required to use special tools and technology to complete the project. They had to find solutions to obstacles that were thrown up by construction. For example, the swamps around the hunting lodge had to be dried out and filled in before construction could begin. Aqueducts had to be built to supply water to the palace.

Louis XIV made it a yearly tradition to visit the Palace of Versailles during the hunting season. He slept in a windmill at the top of a hill. He also liked the location of the palace, as it was a bit of relief from the heat and dust of Paris.

In the 17th century, the Palace of Versailles was used for diplomacy, literature, arts and military conventions. In addition to its role as a royal residence, it served as an assembly place for international councils.

The Palace of Versailles also served as a place of national government. It was the seat of many events, including the Treaty of Versailles, which humiliated the defeated German Empire and lead indirectly to World War II. In the 19th century, the Palace was assigned a new role, as a museum.

Best Spots at Versailles

The palace is filled with grand apartments, state rooms, and lavish gardens.

The Hall of Mirrors

The Hall of Mirrors is the most important venue at the Chateau de Versailles. It was designed in the 17th and 18th centuries and used for a variety of royal ceremonies. It is a bright and spacious room home to 357 mirrors.

The Hall of Mirrors was designed by architect Jules Hardouin-Mansart. It was completed in 1684. It was a replacement for the former large terrace that opened up into the gardens.

The hall was decorated by the artist Charles Le Brun. He painted thirty compositions for the hall. These paintings depict the political and military victories of Louis XIV during the first 18 years of his reign. The design also incorporates the national emblems of France.

In 1770, Louis XIV and Marie Antoinette were married in the Hall of Mirrors. The king was also proclaimed emperor in the Hall of Mirrors.

Marie-Antoinette's bedroom

Marie Antoinette's bedchamber has pastel colors and delicate floral patterns. Her bed was surrounded by gold railings.

The Orangery

This is a large building that was constructed during the 17th century. It features a gilded cornice, and a large niche containing antique style statues.

Musical Gardens Show

You can enjoy the music and fountains of Versailles during the Musical Gardens Show. These shows are held on Fridays, Saturdays, and Sundays. There are additional fees for these special events. https://en.chateauversailles.fr/news/shows/fountains-shows-and-musical-gardens

Queen's Hamlet

During the French Revolution, Queen's Hamlet was abandoned. The buildings were left to rot, but with the help of John Rockefeller in the 1930s, parts of the hamlet were restored. Today, the buildings are quaint and photogenic.

The hamlet was built for Queen Marie Antoinette to escape the formalities of the Palace. It is an artificial village built to replicate an 18th-century Norman village. The buildings include a reception area and the Queen's house. The house is built of two rustic buildings connected by a covered gallery.

Inside the house are private chambers, salons, a kitchen, a billiard room, and a backgammon room. The upper level contains a large living room with a spiral staircase leading to a second floor. The building is decorated with tapestries in Swiss style.

The hamlet also had a farm, sheep, vineyards, fields, and a dairy. A barn, dovecote, and mill were part of the building scheme. The hamlet was called the Hameau de la Reine, a French term meaning "Happy Place." It was built on land outside the Palace of Versailles. It was Marie Antoinette's happy place. She wanted a real working farm in the palace, not just a farm made up of a few buildings.

The Kings apartment

Louis XIV believed that he was the center of the universe. Hence, he called his apartment "the apartment of the planets". Each room in the apartment was dedicated to one of the seven planets. Unfortunately they are not opened for unaccompanied visits.

'This visit requires a Passport ticket or a Trianon and Marie-Antoinette's Estate ticket (which you can purchase directly on site for 12 euro).'

TOP TIP: Picnic in Saint Antony, a park between the Palace of Versailles and the two Trianon palaces. This site has a spectacular view of the Lake of the Swiss Guards. You can also enjoy a variety of activities, such as paddle boating, kayaking, and water skiing.

Visit Disneyland Paris on the cheap

Disneyland Paris is 32 km east of the centre of Paris. The cheapest way to visit Disneyland Paris is to stay in one of the partner hotels: Explorers, Magic Circus, Dream Castle or the Kyrad are all next to each other, there is a free shuttle that collects and drops off every 10-15min from morning until the parks close. Kyriad is usually the cheapest but doesn't have a pool. Entry to the Disney Village is free. If you want to enter the Park, buy your ticket for the park on the website to save 20 euros.
www.disneylandparis.com

Experience a magical river cruise on the cheap

The River Seine has been a vital supply of water that has attracted humans since the Neolithic times. Today the Seine symbolise Parisian romance. There is no better way to see Paris at night than from a boat cruising down the Seine. Many poems and songs took the beautiful Seine as their inspiration and you will see why. The cheapest way to cruise the river is with Vedettes du Pont Neuf. It is impossible to beat on price. The ticket costs 12 euros, you'll recieve a 2 euro discount when booking on their website anytime making it 10 euros. Visit www.vedettesdupont-neuf.com to book.

Climb to Sacré-Cœur

After the Franco-Prussian War ended in 1870, the people of France decided to construct a church in honor of the Sacred Heart in Paris on the butte Montmartre.

This Landmark hilltop white basilica was completed in 1914. Its free to go inside to marvel at the interior mosaics and stained-glass windows. Afterwards walk around pretty Montmartre with its many tourist souvenir shops and cafes.

Sacre Coeur is best visited during daylight hours. The basilica offers sweeping vistas of Paris. You can take pictures outside the basilica, but photography is not allowed inside.

In focus: Montmartre

In the early twentieth century, artists such as Picasso and Modigliani started to settle in Montmartre. They were searching for a place where they could work in a cheap environment. They were also looking for a place with good lighting. The northern part of the hill was also known for its vineyards. In fact, vines have been growing in the Paris region since the Middle Ages.

Montmartre was also a refuge for writers and artists. It was also home to composer Erik Satie, who lived in the town during the first half of the 19th century.

Visit Galeries Lafayette

Galeries Lafayette was built in 1893, when cousins Théophile Bader and Alphonse Kahn decided to establish a novelty store at the corner of rue La Fayette.

Galeries Lafayette is today the second most visited monument in Paris, after the Eiffel Tower. The main hall at Galeries Lafayette is lit up by neo-Byzantine windows. The dome is 43 meters high and is the store's main emblem. You can get an incredible view of Paris from its roof.

We are not going to suggest you spend all your money at this high-end department store but we do suggest you go there to marvel at the Art Nouveau stained-glass dome. After go to the 7th floor to watch a French haute-couture 30-minutes fashion show (advance booking required). Finish off by going to the top floor to enjoy gorgeous views of Paris from the terrace (open in summer only).

Galeries Lafayette also offers a range of free activities. You can take a guided tour of the store, participate in a fitness challenge, or learn how to make macarons. https://haussmann.galeries-lafayette.com/en/funorama/

INSIDER CULTURAL INSIGHT

It is necessary when entering any business to greet workers with either a "Bonjour" or "Bonsoir" if it's the evening. And you should say Merci, au revoir when you leave. Both are important marks of respect.

INSIDER TOP TIP

If you like department stores visit Le Printemps. Located in the 9th Arrondissement, Printemps is one of the most iconic department stores in Paris. This flagship store houses some of the most famous luxury labels and beauty brands in the world. This store has been a part of the French cultural heritage for centuries. It was founded by Jules Jaluzot in 1865. This iconic store is renowned for its gilded domes. It was one of the first stores to install electric lighting in 1888. The store also pioneered the use of window displays. The facade of the building was declared a historical monument. Sculptors such as Carrier-Belleuse were used to decorate the building. The Printemps Haussmann Terrace is one of the best places in Paris to view the city from above. In addition, the department store has a museum dedicated to arts and crafts. The museum is free Thursday evenings between 18:00 and 21:30.

Go Church Hopping

Not only exceptional architecturally and historically, Paris's churches contain exquisite art, artefacts and other priceless treasures. Best of all, entry to general areas within them is, in most cases, free. Some of the most popular are the Basilica of Saint Clotilde, Eglise Saint-Germain, Sacre Coeur, and Saint-Etienne-du-Mont. Each one has its own unique charm, making them an essential stop on your Paris itinerary.

First you must visit 13th century **Sainte-Chapelle** to see its mind-blowing stained glass windows.

Notre-Dame Cathedral

Founded in the year 1163, the Notre Dame Cathedral in Paris is one of the most famous symbols of the city. It is also a UNESCO World Heritage Site. It was one of the tallest structures in Europe at the time of its construction.

Notre Dame Cathedral was built upon the site of a pagan temple. It was designed by the architect Jean de Chelles and was completed by his son Jean Ravy. They began building Notre-Dame in 1163 and completed 170 years later, it's a prime example of gothic style, with its rose windows and massive flying buttresses.

You can still visit Cathédrale Notre-Dame de Paris from outside even after the fire.

Eglise St-Germain

Located in the Saint-Germain-des-Pres district, the Eglise Saint-Germain-des-Pres is one of the oldest churches in Paris. It was founded in 543 by King Childebert, who built a monastery close to the Seine to keep out of the floods. The abbey was destroyed several times during the French Revolution, and parts were in danger of collapsing by the 1820s.

In the late 19th century, the abbey was restored. The church is now one of Paris's best examples of Gothic architecture. The facade of the church features 54 Corinthian columns, as well as reliefs of the Ten Commandments. The sanctuary features a marble group representing Mary Magdalene in heaven.

The interior of the church is a blend of Gothic and Renaissance artwork. It features a vaulted choir area and a High Gothic cathedral. It is also home to the famous 18th-century Clicquot organ. The church hosts free organ recitals and daily Mass.

Basilica of Saint Clotilde

Located in Paris' 7th arrondissement, Basilica of Saint Clotilde is a basilica church. It was built in 1846-1857 and is best known for its twin spires. It was declared a minor basilica by Pope Leo XIII in 1896.

The facade of the Basilica of Saint Clotilde features sculptures of saints, including Clovis and Clotilde. It is the first church in Paris to be built in a neo-gothic style. It was designed by Cologne architect F. C. Gau.

The interior of the basilica is modest but well-lit. There are side-aisles on either side of the nave. Stained-glass windows depict both the Old and New Testaments.

The chapel on the western side of the cathedral contains fine paintings by Lenepveu. It also features a statue of St. Clotilde, a daughter of Chilperic, the fifth century king of Burgundy. The statue is leaned against a pillar at the entrance.

Saint-Etienne-du-Mont

The Saint-Etienne-du-Mont church is also one of the oldest churches in Paris. It was built in the 1500s. It was built on the grounds of an abbey that was dedicated to Sainte-Geneviève. Sainte-Genevieve was one of the most popular saints in Paris. She was a woman from Nanterre who became a nun at the age of 15. She was a popular saint for her visions. She was also known for her prayers to divert the Hun army from Paris. Her tomb is in the church.

Saint-Sulpice

Located in the 6th arrondissement of Paris, the Saint-Sulpice is one of the most beautiful and oldest churches in Paris. Its facade is a unique combination of Baroque and Neoclassical styles. It has a large organ that has been rebuilt several times in the past. It is also one of the oldest Roman Catholic churches in Paris. The Saint-Sulpice organ is one of the largest organs in France. It has 6,500 pipes and five layered keyboards. It was rebuilt in the 19th century by Aristide Cavaille-Coll. He also built the organ at the Notre Dame Cathedral.

The church was used as a setting for a scene in the movie The Da Vinci Code. A character named Eymard was preaching about the Sacred Heart of Jesus. He was also speaking about the ingratitude of humans.

Visit Icons

Père Lachaise Cemetery

Père Lachaise Cemetery is a vast tree-lined burial site with many famous people buried there including Oscar Wilde, Jim Morrison , Maria Callas, Edith Piaf and Sandra Bernhardt. The Cemetery is Open daily from 8am-7pm. The main gates are located on the Boulevard de Menilmontant.

The cemetery was designed to accommodate the wealthy Parisians. It is known for its beautiful tombstones and dramatic statues. In the upper levels, you can enjoy panoramic views of Paris.

If you are a Emily in Paris fan you'll recognise Père Lachaise Cemetery from when Luc and Emily lunch there together.

Go Thrift shopping

The French fashion industry exploded in the late 19th and early 20th century. In 1925 Coco Chanel revolutionized Paris fashion and then the world's. But you don't need to have Chanel money to enjoy Parisian fashion at its best. Thrift stores also known as charity shops or second hand shops are full of chic bargains in Paris if you know where to look. Marais is nice for vintage and thrift shopping. Also Boulevard Saint-Michel has awesome places. If you like flea markets, Marché aux Puces is a MUST!

The Star Thrift Store in Paris opened in 1994. There are three stores in the city, including one in the heart of Le Marais. They all have a lot of stock and are popular among Parisians. They offer a great selection of clothes, with prices averaging between EUR5 and 15 euros.

The Norma Thrift Shop is owned by a mother and daughter. It's located next to a former Colette boutique and has a lot of red carpet-worn clothing. You can find designer pieces, including Neverfull Vuitton, at very low prices.

The Vintage 77 shop is a local favorite. Located in the 20th arrondissement, it's a great spot to find vintage clothing at great prices. They also sell vintage designer items, including Chanel jackets and bags.

Google for the most expensive area in Paris (currently the 6th Arrondissement: Saint-Germain-des-Prés). Navigate there on Google maps. Then put the American term Thrift store into Google Maps. Start with the most expensive areas and work your way through until the middle-tier ones. You will be surprised what you find in Paris with a bit of patience!

INSIDER TOP TIPS

1. If you love hunting down bargains head to San-Francisco Book Co. It is an English book store in Paris. If you take the time to search, you're certain to find some gems and possibly even valuable first editions! Address: 17 Rue Monsieur le Prince
2. The first day of les soldes is always the best day to shop. During the first day of the sale, the crowds are ferocious and prices are reduced 30-40 percent. After the first rush, the selection narrows and prices drop further.
3. You can also find a variety of samples sales. The Arlettie sample sales site is one example. This company has multiple locations in Paris and organizes sample sales for high-end fashion brands.

Best Places to Buy Second Hand Chanel in Paris

Buying a classic Chanel bag is a lifelong dream for many. Although Chanel is a luxury brand, the prices are more reasonable in France. Buying second hand even more so. The bag can be super cheap if you view it as an investment you could resell for more than you paid.

There are several Chanel second hand shops in Paris. One of the most famous ones is called Monogram Paris. This showroom offers a wide selection of luxury items.

Another shop with a good selection is Opulence Luxury. It specializes in second hand luxury accessories and carries Chanel, Louis Vuitton, Hermes, and more.

Another shop to look into is Les 3 Marches De Catherine B. This is a tiny boutique that has been in business since 1994. It is located in the Saint Germain des Pres neighborhood. It specializes in Chanel jackets in mint condition. It also offers a 30% discount on all articles during sales.

TOP TIP: Save 20% shopping

Buy your Chanel bag in Paris. You'll save on the import costs and you can claim the Value added tax back at the airport. Ask for tax relief documentation when you buy. You need to stay there less than six months and be a NON-EU resident to qualify.

Pack a picnic

The cost of eating out can quickly add up in Paris. For a meal that doesn't break the bank, prepare your own picnic to enjoy in a park with a blanket and a bottle of wine. Picnics are a favourite pastime of Parisians, so grab some wine cheese and bread and head to the bank of the seine, canal saint martin, or almost any parc and just enjoy the the scenery.

The French capital has some of the best-kept parks in the world, and it doesn't cost a thing to pull up one of the free chairs and relax for a while.

Jardin du Carrousel before Le Louvre is adorned with endless statues, Jardin du Luxembourg lies in front of a palace of the same name, while the view of the Eiffel Tower from **Parc du Champ de Mars** is unforgettable. It is my absolute favourite garden in Paris. Created by regent Queen Marie de Médici in 1612 to complement her new residence Palais du Luxembourg. It has been the seat of the French Senate since 1958.

Buttes Chaumont Parc is one of the most beautiful parks in Paris. Grab a bottle of wine (and an opener) then head to the park and lay on a blanket, there's really no better way to waste a few hours.

Parc floral de Paris is a gorgeous park filled with over 3,000 flower species. It's 2€ entry, but worth every penny.

Parc des Buttes-Chaumont, a giant park north of the city. The park is popular among locals and is the perfect place to have a picnic and observe the local life. It also features a Roman Pavilion and Gustave Eiffel's suspension bridge. Another attraction in the park is the Grand Rex theatre. This iconic Art Deco landmark is home to the world's largest movie theatre. It is also home to a shrine dedicated to Saint Genevieve. This place has an amazing view of the city.

Another must-see attraction in Parc des Buttes-Chaumont is the Temple de la Sibylle, which is located on a rocky cliff. It is a beautiful structure that overlooks Sacre Coeur. It was inspired by the Temple of Vesta in Tivoli, Italy. This temple is free to visit and has excellent views of the city.

INSIDER MONEY SAVING TIP

If you're at a loss for what cheese or wine to buy from supermarkets try a a cheap rosé, a fresh beaujolais, or a lovely red from the South: Langue, Provence, Gaillac are the best. For cheese you can't go wrong with a sharp gorgonzola or a Mont d'or laced with truffle. Team with a fresh white baguette.

Explore Paris' Street art

Works of art in the streets define Paris. Colorful murals and graffiti art are displayed throughout the city. Murals sometimes cover

up entire buildings and symbolize recent and historical events and topics. Here are the best places to spot the most incredible urban canvasses:

- Oberkampf. This colourful neighbourhood is renowned for its vibrant walls and range of high profile street artists.

- Belleville. - Despite being a working class neighborhood, Belleville has become a hot spot for art. In fact, the Belleville district is home to some of the most spectacular street art in Paris. The neighborhood is also home to some of the city's most creative artists, who make their creative studios and studio spaces available to the public.

- Place Igor Stravinsky - home to the world's largest stencil graffiti. It features a fountain designed by French artist Jean Tinguely and a mural by French street artist Jef Aerosol.

- Butte aux Cailles - ephemeral pieces and monumental murals. It's also a great place for drinks and a nice dinner. The most interesting street art piece here is Children on Lamppost, which is located on the Rue de l'Esperance. It depicts children wearing medieval helmets. This artwork is one of the most popular in the neighborhood.
- Auberviliers Street - The street is also home to many large murals, making it a prime spot for urban art lovers. The Boulevard 13 Project is a collaborative effort between 22 different artists. The artists have designed thirty-two murals, which are large and vibrant. The murals have been painted in a modern-contemporary style, capturing the social and cultural aspects of the city.
- Jardin Grands-Moulin - One of the most popular attractions is a giant mural of a man and woman kissing on a wall that overlooks the park. The mural was painted in 2010 by local street artists. It's one of the most famous street art murals in France.
- The Confettier - The cobblestone enclaves of Montmartre and Le Marais. The best way to see it all is to stroll the narrow paths and narrow alleys of these two

neighborhoods. You'll be treated to a parade of the good, the bad, and the ugly.

Explore the Best Markets

Marché Bastille

Markets are a fun and eye-opening plunge into local Parisian culture and, unless you succumb to the persistent vendors, it will cost you nothing. Start off by visiting the oldest food market in Paris: Marché des Enfants Rouges it dates back to 1628 and is packed full of delicacies and samples!

Then go to the lively market: Marché d'Aligre. A typical French farmer's market with an abundance of fresh products. You can find organic and locally sourced products here. It's open most days of the week. The closed section has more premium products.

The best food market is undoubtably: Marché Bastille. Here you'll find the best cheese, charcuterie, and olives in Paris.

The most traditional food market is Marché Mouffetard. Visit on Sundays to enjoy a bustling atmosphere, great music and cheap eats.

Visit the Modern market: Les Halles, Paris's central fresh food market. It was demolished in 1971 and replaced into a modern shopping mall built largely underground and directly connected to the metro.

Les Puces de Saint-Ouen

The most famous flea market in Paris is at Porte de Clignancourt, officially called Les Puces de Saint-Ouen, but locals call it Les Puces (The Fleas). It covers seven hectares and is the largest antique market in the world. It's lovely to rummage through and a very good place to find fine old antiques. There are over 200 stalls with an eclectic range of wares. It attracks over 180,000 visitors each weekend. It's renowned for its quaint charm and friendly vendors. You can find vintage clothing, handmade jewelry and other items at its Marche Malassis and Marche le Passage. If you're a bargain hunter, you'll love the flea market's stalls displaying designer goods from various eras.

Visit Rungis International Market

The Rungis International Market is the world's largest wholesale food market. It covers 232 hectares. It is one of the most famous markets in France.

The market is open to visitors on the second Friday of every month. This is the time when local and foreign restaurants stock up on fresh produce.

The Rungis market has five main sections. These sections are the wholesale, the marine, the fruit and vegetable, the decorative and the school sector. Visit for a unique free experience.

Moulin Rouge

When the Moulin Rouge opened on 6 October 1889, The aim was to allow the very rich to come and 'slum it' in a fashionable district, Montmartre.

Today the Moulin Rouge is a vastly overpriced tourist trap. Tickets start at $120 and there's no work around. Instead you could go to watch Free Comedy at Laughing Matters at La Java

Address: 105 rue du Faubourg du Temple, Paris 10 th.

If you are yearning to see a cabernet show in Paris, go around the corner to La Nouvelle Eve. It's a smaller venue so it feels like you're more involved. Seats cost €69 which includes half a bottle of champagne

Go to one of the cities best cabarets

Belleville is home to one of the city's best cabarets, the Zebre de Belleville. It is located at 63 Boulevard de Belleville. This cabaret is a traditional Parisian cabaret. Tickets are 27.50€.

If you're interested in acrobats Le Zebre de Belleville as holds a circus workshop for a short duration on a Wedensday that runs from 2pm through to 3.30pm and is a cost of around €14.'

Go to Free Concerts in Paris

Go to the Italian Cultural Institute. This place is located near the Pompidou Center. The Italian Cultural Institute will offer free operettas and operetta concerts. https://iicparigi.esteri.it/iic_parigi/it/

You can also attend a free classical music concert in Paris organized by Radio France. You can find out more about this event on the Radio France website. https://www.radiofrance.fr/

Another free concert that you can enjoy in Paris is the Atelier Concert Series. This event is held every Sunday evening at 17h30. It will give you the chance to hear talented musicians from all over the world. You can also visit the Atelier Series website to learn more. https://www.acparis.org/music-a-arts-76181/concerts-a-recitals-659/atelier-concerts-29401

Get Cheap Opera Tickets in Paris

Opera Garnier

Opera de Paris offers flash sales online on Wednesdays at noon. These sales are available for some of the most popular shows in Paris including at Palais Garnier and Opéra Bastille. https://www.operadeparis.fr/en

Opera Bastille is the home of some of the most spectacular performances in the world. Tickets for performances there can cost as little as EUR5 (for a ticket to a Sunday chamber music concert) and can get as expensive as EUR150. If you are planning a trip to Paris and want to take in the show, you should book your tickets as early as possible.

Go to Free Outdoor Cinema Screenings

During the summer months, Paris is a hotspot for open air cinema. These festivals are held around the city's most iconic monuments, and are often free.

One of the most popular open air cinemas in Paris is at Parc de la Villette. This venue screens films nightly. The largest screen in the park is impressive. Moreover, you can rent deck chairs for EUR7. You can even picnic on the lawn.

The French senate gardens are another popular site for outdoor movie screenings. This spot is particularly beautiful at sunrise and sunset. You can enjoy lush plants and interesting sculptures while you watch the show.

Another great choice is La Villette cinema festival. This event runs from mid-July to mid-September. In addition to being a popular summer hangout, La Villette is one of the most budget friendly places to see an outdoor movie in Paris. The cost of a general admission ticket is EUR5.

In the summer you can watch a free film under the stars in Parc de la Villlette www.lavillette.com

Go Swimming

One of the most popular swimming pools in Paris is the Josephine Baker pool. The pool is located on a barge on the Seine River. It was built to mirror swimming in the Seine. It is open to the public in the summer. The view of the Seine from the barge is breathtaking. It is also the perfect place to unwind and take a refreshing dip.

Another swimming pool that is worth visiting is the Henry de Mon-therlant pool. It is located on the left bank of the Seine. It has a 25 x 15 meter swimming pool, and is open 7 days a week from 6.30am to 10pm.

Enjoy Free Jazz

If you like Jazz, visit Cave du 38 Riv'Jazz in Le Marais they have free admission on Mondays, Thursdays and Fridays.

Go to a gallery open-ing

Artnet has a daily listings of FREE gallery openings in Paris.
http://www.artnet.com/events/paris/

Watch football on the cheap

PSG tickets often start at $120 with an average price closer to $138 but you can get them much cheap. Here you have tickets advertised for $50: - https://seatpick.com/paris-saint-germain-psg-tickets.

Aux Sports is a great place to watch a game and they have cheap drinks. Address: 2 Rue des Morillons.

Visit Canal Saint-Martin

Whether you're looking for a quiet place to escape, a great view, or a trendy place to spend a cheap night out, Canal Saint-Martin offers the perfect escape.

The Canal Saint-Martin is a small waterway that links the Seine to the Canal du Ourcq in eastern France. It was built in the 19th century by Napoleon I as a way to provide Paris with more fresh water.

It has seven iron footbridges, as well as a mysterious underground vault that served as a backdrop to a few films. The best way to explore the canal is to go by bike. There's a wide range of restaurants, bars, and cafes along the banks of the canal serving cheap drinks at night.

Visit Bercy Village

Located in the east of Paris, Bercy Village is a shopping and entertainment district which was once a vineyard. A large park, Parc de Bercy, is one of the main attractions. It includes two arching footbridges, a mini-vineyard, a sun porch, and themed flower beds. In addition to these, there are several gardens that offer lovely walkways, ponds, and century-old trees.

Visit Pont Neuf

Pont Neuf is the oldest standing bridge in Paris and is a major landmark for the city. It spans the Seine and connects the Right Bank and Ile de la Cite. It was constructed in the early 17th century over a number of predecessor bridges.

Construction of the bridge began under King Henri III in the year 1578 and was completed in 1598 during the reign of Henry IV. The bridge originally contained houses, but Henry IV decided to remove them when it was completed. The king was worried that the buildings would block the view of the Louvre.

The Pont Neuf is also known as the Old bridge. It was built according to ancient Roman design standards. Today, there are several architectural features on the bridge. There are 381 stone mascarons which are replicas of original renaissance artworks. In addition, the bridge also contains a bronze statue of Henry IV dating from 1818. Another 19th century architectural feature is the La Samaritaine building, which honors an original pump that once adorned the bridge.

Visit The Champs-El-ysees

Known for its beautiful architecture and chic shopping, the Champs-Elysees are one of the most popular Paris attractions. This area is home to the famous Arc de Triomphe and the tomb of the unknown soldier. It also attracts many tourists during Bastille Day and the Christmas season. There are many shops, restaurants, and cafes to choose from.

A trip to the Champs-Elysees will allow you to experience French culture while shopping, drinking, and dining. The area is filled with luxury stores and restaurants, and there are plenty of options for less expensive establishments as well. The area is also home to a number of theatres and performing arts theatres. The Champs-Elysees is also the place where the world-famous Tour de France ends. The street is also filled with festive lights and music shows. You can also see a fashion runway show in the area.

Champs-Elysees is one of the best places to see the flame of liberty. This monument is an exact replica of the torch from the Statue of Liberty in New York. It also symbolizes the friendship between France and the United States. It is best visited in the evening.

A trip to Champs-Elysees is not complete without a visit to the Arc de Triomphe. The monument was commissioned by Napoleon Bonaparte to commemorate French military victories.

Do Free yoga

Working out in Paris is expensive. Prices range from 15€-25€ per session, which can quickly add up. Thankfully, You can find free yoga sessions by visiting - http://www.freeinParis.com/affordable-yoga-Paris/

Visit the oldest tree in Paris

Place Rene Viviani located in the Latin Quarter is a charming garden. This green space is one of the best viewing spots for the Notre Dame Cathedral.

This small park is home to the oldest tree in Paris. It is a robinia pseudoacacia, which has been standing for 400 years. The tree receives special attention from the city's urban gardeners.

The park has several comfortable chairs scattered around. When the weather is nice, roses bloom. The square also features a modern bronze fountain designed by Georges Jeanclos.

Walk Coulee Verte Rene-Dumont

Do as the locals do and walk Coulee Verte Rene-Dumont. You'll get a unique view of Paris. This bucolic path is a great way to escape the city. It is located in the 12th arrondissement of Paris.

This 4.5 km walk offers panoramas of the city. It is also a popular spot for Sunday walks. The walk is divided into three sections. The western section is open to pedestrians only. The eastern section is reserved for cyclists. The walkway is accessed via stairways in Avenue Daumesnil and Daumesnil. It takes about an hour and a half to walk.

People watch outside a café

The French are a passionate race and watching them go about their daily lives is one of the best things you can do in Paris. Get yourself comfy outside one of the city's omnipresent cafés, sit back and watch the world go by.

Escape the crowds

Paris's 2.1 million inhabitants are squeezed into 40 square miles so escaping the crowds may seem like an oxymoron, but its possible even with the throngs of tourists. If you are easily overwhelmed by crowds visit the obvious attractions as early as possible, peak people flow is 11 am to 5 pm so get up early to enjoy the attractions serenely. Luckily Paris also has many hidden gems that aren't commercialised or too crowded most of the time. Here are the best for you to explore:

1. Rue Cremieux is a small pedestrian street that's lined with houses painted in bright colours. Visit at noon when the sun lights up the brightly colored houses.

2. The <u>Parc des Buttes-Chaumont</u> was created out of an abandoned quarry. It opened in 1867 and is a great place to relax away from the crowds.

3. As mentioned, the terrace at Printemps Department store offers amazing panoramic views of Paris. Take the elevator to Cafe Déli-Cieux.

4. The often overlooked Rue Mouffetard is one of the best market streets in the whole of Paris and relatively quiet before 10am.

5. Monet's Garden in Giverny.

6. The castles in the Loire Valley

7. You can do a day trip by train to Brussels (1.5 hours each way) or Luxembourg (2.5 hours each way).

8. La Promenade Plantée is an old subway station/stop turned into a beautiful 4Km walking park that takes you through several neighbourhoods and is amazing.

9. Parc sceaux: another gorgeous park with a gorgeous chateau. The best cherry blossoms in Paris area.

10. Musee de Cluny, which is dedicated to the dark arts of the Middle Ages and is housed in a Gothic mansion.

11.Visit the Tombe of Vincent Van-Gogh. An hour outside Pairs you'll find Auvers. It's home to a church that was painted by Vincent Van Gogh in 1890. The painting is now on display at the Musee d'Orsay in Paris and is up there with 'The Sunflowers' in terms of beauty. Auvers also houses the cemetery where the painter shot himself. His grave lies next to the grave of his beloved. It is surrounded by ivy and sunflowers symbolically representing his love.

12. If you want to explore a lavender field hop a train to Avignon or Aix-en-Provence.

INSIDER CULTURAL INSIGHT

Parisians haven't endeared themselves to French people living outside the capital. They are known as "Parigot, tête de veau" The Parisian is pig-headed". The literal translation sounds sweeter The Parisian calf-headed.

Get something totally for free

You could furnish an entire apartment pretty decently with all the things people are giving away in Paris.

If you find you need to buy something, whether that be a charger or torch in Paris check free stuff in Paris sites before you buy. You can often find incredible freebies here that will cost you only the time to pick them up. Here is the best free stuff group in Paris: https://www.facebook.com/groups/1183771798346724/

Perfect PHOTO SPOTS

- The black and white columns at Palais Royal
- The golden gate at Petit-Palais
- Trocadero, overlooking the Eiffel Tower
- Pont Alexandre III and Pont de Bir-Hakeim both have fantastic views of the Eiffel Tower for photos
- Pigalle basketball court
- Place des Vosges.

Not super cheap but loved

Atelier des lumieres

Atelier des lumieres is one of the most moving art experiences you can ever have. Classic paintings are elaborated with modern projections, music and style. Among others, the work of Klimt comes alive and unfolded with drama and emotion. It costs €14.50 to enter. Don't forget to visit the mirror room and a studio room under the stairs for a meditative experience.

Go inside Arc de Triomphe

The Arc de Triomphe the largest arch in the world. It is a Neoclassical take on the triumphal arch style of the Roman Empire. It is located near the Seine River, in the center of a circular roadway on the busiest road in Paris. It is located on the western edge of the Avenue des Champs-Elysees.

The Arc de Triomphe was built between 1806 and 1836. It is made of light grey limestone and guarded by metal spikes. The Arc de Triomphe de l'Etoile is also a museum. This museum tells the story of the construction of the Arc de Triomphe de l'Etoile.

You can climb to the top of the arch and visit the musuem by purchasing an elevator ticket online. The price is EUR13. https://www.paris-arc-de-triomphe.fr/en/

Musee de l'Orangerie

The Orangerie was reopened in 2006 after a comprehensive renovation. Among its permanent collections are works by Monet, Picasso, Matisse, and Modigliani. The museum is also known for its Water Lilies rooms.

Monet's Water Lilies are displayed in two large oval rooms. Each panel measures two meters high and depicts the peaceful setting of the Water Gardens at Giverny. These paintings were only completed a few months after the artist's death. They change with the light. They are an example of Monet's unique illusion of light. Tickets are 12.50 euro.

The Catacombs of Paris

The Paris Catacombs are located south of the main city center. You can reach the site via Paris Metro trains M-4 and M-6. You can also take a bus. The bus stop is located on Denfert Rochereau av.

A timed ticket is a good idea, as it ensures you don't have to wait for a long time. You can purchase tickets at the site on the day you visit.

If you want to get up close and personal with the bones, you should consider getting a guided tour. Tour guides can take you to deeper areas of the Catacombs. You can also buy audio books, which are available for a small fee. Tickets are expensive at 29 euros.

The Musee d'Orsay

Originally a train station, the Musee d'Orsay is now one of the top things to do in Paris. You can expect to see a lot of impressionist and Post-Impressionist works at the Musee d'Orsay, including works by Vincent Van Gogh, Edgar Degas and Monet. It also has a variety of other collections, including photography and sculptures.

The top floor is also home to one of the best museum cafes in Paris. You can enjoy a view of the Seine, and you catch a glimpse of the Sacre-Coeur basilica.

You can also visit the museum on the first Sunday of every month otherwise tickets are 16 euros.

Food and drink hacks

Eat at the cafe under napoleons tomb

For just 11€ per person you can eat under napoleons tomb. The cafe is relatively unknown and only open from 11-2 pm. It's run by nuns and all the money goes to help the needy. To enter, if you're standing in front of the building it's around the left side, pass the flower vendor.

Address: Musée de l'Armée, 129 Rue de Grenelle

Eat in the double digit arrondissements

The best way to find the most affordable Paris food is to head for the less crowded areas. This includes residential neighborhoods, where a number of small restaurants cater to locals. The food is usually cheaper and the service is better.

Appreciate the local flavours without paying gourmet restaurant prices

Go to supermarkets and bakeries! Buy meat, cheese & bread in supermarkets. Everything will be delicious. Avoid the touristy looking bakeries and try to wander down a sidestreet and find a smaller one catering to locals.

Visit "Buoillion" restaurants

'A bouillon is a traditional spacious restaurant that usually serves traditional French cuisine, in particular a Bouillon (broth), which has provided the name for this class of restaurants.' You can eat French Cuisine there from 10/15 euro.

€5 pizzas

Pizza Populare = 5€ pizzas

Best crepes

The menu at Creperie Genia is small but consists of deliciously sweet and savory crepes. The crepes can be eaten in the cafe or ordered to go. The restaurant is located on the Seine bank.

Try Workaday bistros

If you are looking for a cheap Paris restaurant, you can try La Bouchonnier. The restaurant offers both meat and vegetarian meals for just a few euros. This restaurant is one of the last old-fashioned workaday bistros in the city. It is located in the 3rd arrondissement.

Cheap burgers

The menu at Le Camion Qui Fume has classic burgers. Their sandwiches start at around EUR7. They also offer banh mi sandwiches.

Go for Lunch menu's (Menu du jour)

Lots of restaurants also have lunch menus on weekdays so you can get a 2 course meal for 10-15€pp.

Download the app Dojo

It tells you price range and distance for Paris restaurants.

Visit a Middle Ages pâtisserie

Le Moulin de la Vierge on rue Saint Dominique is a pâtisserie shop that's been open since the Middle Ages.

Sports bars

If you want to drink while watching sports, Formula Match is a great place to go. Beers start at EUR3, and you can get a burger of your choice and a pint for EUR12. The small terrace is a great place to hang out and watch the game.

Best bang for your buck all-you-can-eat's

Paris offers an array of bargain all you can eat restaurants with lunches for $15. These are the best three:

1. Buffet Sentier - the all you can eat sushi lunch includes desserts which is a real plus

2. Dim Sum House Restaurant. They offer an all-you-can-eat menu in which you can find all of the

3. Restaurant Hao Hao Sushi. High quality all-you-can-eat Japanese restaurant. Service is fast and everything is delicious.

All you can eat buffets are a great way to stock on on nutritious food while travelling. Dishes like fish are normally expensive especially in cities, but here you can chow down on your omega 3's for much less. I know friends who take Tupperware with them to take some snacks away, personally I don't as its not ethical and karma is real. Don't drink much water or eat bread and you'll get more than your money's worth.

Where to Find the Best Macarons in Paris

For cheap, delicious macarons go to the bakery Maison Landemaine, about 12 of them around the city -the one at 56 rue de Clichy is amazing - they are very colourful, delicious and less expensive than the Michelin star chefs options (and better in my opinion).

Mulot, which is located in the sixth arrondissement is famous for its wide variety of flavors. Another great place to find macarons in Paris is Carl Marletti. This cafe is run by a patissier who is a pioneer of macarons. His cafe is located in the Latin Quarter and offers a selection of original desserts. You can also enjoy coffee cremeux or Carioca.

You can also buy them for as little as a couple of euros at McDonald's.

Desperate for Macarons?

The storied macarons of Ladurée offer delivery in less than 90min in Paris! But the price is as you'd expect - expensive.

The Best Cheese Shops in Paris

Specialty cheese shops are called fromageries in France. As mentioned above, one of the best cheese shops in Paris is La Fromagerie. This shop is a family owned business, and they have been selling cheese for over 50 years. They are very knowledgeable about the cheeses they sell, and can advise you on the best cheeses from France. They have a large selection of cheeses, including classics like Comte. They also offer special cheese platters, and are open for cheese tastings.

La Ferme du Faubourg also offers professional workshops and classes. They are also known for their cheese fondue.

Another great cheese shop in Paris is Fromagerie Quatrehomme. This cheese shop is located in the 7th Arrondissement. It is owned by a fourth generation family member who has been selling cheese since 1953. They carry a wide variety of cheeses, and also sell whisky and other gourmet odds and ends. They are open from 9 am to 8 pm, and are very friendly. They have won awards for their cheeses, and are a great place to go for cheese tastings.

Laurent Dubois has several cheese shops in Paris. He is known for his sheep milk cheeses from the Pyrenees, and has won the Meilleur Ouvrier de France (M.O.F.) title in 2011 and 2014. He is also well-known for his house-made creations. They are available in his shop on Boulevard Saint-Germain.

Go to Oyster Happy Hours in Paris

There are three oyster growing regions in France. These are Arcachon, Marennes-Oleron, and Cancale. The oysters in these areas are more robust and more expensive than the ones in the other two regions.

There are oyster happy hours in Paris all year long. Some restaurants serve oysters with sauce mignonette, which is made with shallots, red wine vinegar, and various seasonings.

You can find oysters in all shapes and sizes at Le Dome. This Montparnasse cafe dates back to the year 1898 and still has a wonderful atmosphere. The oysters are grouped by size and weight, and ordered by number.

There are also oyster happy hours at Opium and La Cabane. This restaurant is located between upscale art galleries in the 6th arrondissement. The oysters are only EUR1 during happy hours. You can find over a dozen varieties of oysters here. They are served raw on half shell, usually with lemon wedges.

Enjoy Main courses under 10 euros

Baguettes, Croissants, Macarons. Paris is a bread and pastry lover's dream but there are also incredible omelettes and Falafel. Not to mention mouthwatering crepes. It's actually quite hard to have a bad meal in Paris, but it's easy to have an overpriced one. Fill your stomach without emptying your wallet in Paris by trying these local restaurants with mains under $10.

Note: Download the offline map on Google maps, (instructions 1. go to app 2. select offline apps in the left sidebar 3. go to the area you want to download 4. click download). Then simply type the restaurant names in to navigate, add it to your favourites by clicking the star icon so you can see where the cheap eats are when you're out and about to avoid wasting your money at hyped tourist joints)

Bouillon Chartier is an authentic Parisian restaurant with really good prices for local dishes, with mains starting at €8

Fixed menu at Le Ciel de Paris.
Great views and surprisingly good food. Menu "Gourmand" 35 €. Book a table at Le Ciel de Paris in Paris.

Le Procope
Ignore the $$$ on **Le Procope**. Go early and you can choose from the fixed menu. The history of the building is amazing. Walk around the place while waiting for your food. They have Voltaire's desk and a letter by Marie Antoinette before her execution.

Le Troquet – It is in the 15th right by the Sevres-LeCouree Metro stop. It's a local bistro with GREAT food. We strongly recommend having the cheese course here and the Vanilla Souffle is considered the best in the world by many.

Bistrot Victoires is one of my favourite hidden gems in Paris Good french mains for 12-14€ and cheap house carafes of wine.

Maison Blanche
 quite a touristy area near Notre Dame but the food is good and it's cheap And the place has a great atmosphere Would totally recommend Address is 21 Rue de la Huchette, 75005

Au Petit Grec on rue Mouffetard is so good, 5 or so euros for a full galette (but be prepared to wait a while in line) For takeaway street crêpes,

Cartouche Café: A small french bistro near bercy village. Chalkboard menu that changes daily, incredibly delicious in EVERY sense of the word. (if you go get the chocolate kitsu for dessert you will not regret squeezing it in)

Maison Maison: café/bar located in the wall of the seine near pont neuf, an excellent place for a wine break during the day. beautiful view of the seine.

Frenchies to go: A sandwich shop by chef Frenchie, they do to go so you can take your sandwich & sit in a park/picnic on the seine if you'd like.

Happy nouille: A Chinese soup noodle place, tiny yet efficient. They hand pull noodles for every bowl so you're getting fresh noods everytime.

MELT BBQ: The chef trained in dallas texas, they offer a variety of beef and pork. I love the loaded fries with brisket.

CANTINA: Spanish/Mexican food, the menu changes sometimes but all their food is packed full of flavor, also has vegetarian options.

Paname brewing company: A brewery on the north end of canal saint martin. Great for beer lovers, they have a full menu and a gorgeous patio.

Holybelly has two amazing Aussie-inspired cafés (but with some classic French ingredients). Holybelly 5 does classic breakfast like pancakes, eggs, even Vegemite on toast, and Holybelly 19 does seasonal breakfast plates which are DELICIOUS. Try the mini donuts with dulce de leche.

Breizh Café
Cheap delicious Crêperie.

Bistro Victoiries
Late-night French food on the cheap.

Krishna Bhavan Restaurant
Vegetarian cheap Indian.

A La Biche Au Bois
Cheaper than most Parisian bistros and the food is better.

Chez Gladines
Great French food and huge portions! (beware, you REALLY have to be hungry to finish most of the dishes here).

Chez Shen
One of the best Chinese places in Paris and super cheap.

Happy Nouilles
A Chinese soup noodle place, tiny yet efficient. They hand pull noodles for every bowl so you're getting fresh noodles everytime. Delicious, inexpensive noddles and very quick.

Urfa Durum
Fantastic, authentic, cheap Kurdish sandwich. I recommend the lamb.

Le Comptoir de l'Arc
next to the Arc de Triomphe for good lunch/dinner for around €12

(v. authentic experience, only open on weekdays).

Cartouche Café
A small french bistro near bercy village. Chalkboard menu that changes daily, incredibly delicious in EVERY sense of the word. (if you go get the chocolate kitsu for dessert you will not regret it).

TOP FOODIE TIPS

- **Carette** has the best croissants in Paris.
- **Angelina** is a must for hot chocolate
- The Latin Quarter has loads of restaurants that offer lunch and dinner fixed price menus, perfect if you're on a budget
  There's a chain café called Brioche Doree and they have the GREATEST muffin - it's called a Nutella Muffinoiserie. A hybrid between a muffin and a croissant, with Nutella inside.
- **Ten bells bakery**: bread bread bread, come here and feast on the bread.

INSIDER HISTORICAL INSIGHT

Visit the original road to Rome: Rue Mouffetard, one of the oldest streets in Paris. The street takes its name from the River Bièvre which flows beneath it. In medieval times the smell, the moffettes was so strong that the street was name Rue Mouffetard to warn people. Today the smell has been replaced by restaurants selling some of the best cheap eats in Paris.

Best Cinemas in Paris

Some of the best cinemas in Paris include Le Reflet Medicis, Max Linder, La Filmo, Studio 28, La Geode, Le Balzac, Forum Cinema, Cine Sorbonne, Cinema des Champs-Elysees, Filmotheque Quarter Latin, and Cinema de Pantheon.

The Max Linder cinema opened in 1914. Its programme features contemporary and international blockbusters. The cinema also screens documentaries and auteur cinema. It has a panoramic screen and surround sound. The cinema also offers mini-retrospectives of lesser known world cinema directors.

Located in the 7th arrondissement, La Pagode features English-language films and revivals. Its building is modeled after a Chinese pagoda and is designed in a chic, green style. It also has a cool green terrace for tea. It is open daily at 2:00pm and is a popular venue for film noir revivals.

The Forum Cinema is a 19th-century replica of a pagoda and part screening venue for old movies. Its collection numbers more than 6,500 films. The cinema is also part archive for films featuring Paris.

The Cinema de Pantheon was the first cinema in Paris to show films in their original language. It was also the first cinema to screen foreign films. It was a hotbed of intellectuals and fans of the '7th art'.

In the 1960s, Le Balzac became a favorite haunt of the nouvelle vague directors. Its theater boasts a mock ocean-liner foyer and is decorated in an elegant style. It also awards prizes to the audience according to their votes.

Nightlife

Paris' Nightlife is a mix of traditional cafes, classy nightclubs, dive bars, and music venues. Bar hopping down hectic rue de Lappe or Rue de la Roquette is a good place to start. Other Prime Parisian streets for cheap partying are:

- Rue Princesse, Student and sports bars.

- Rue Vieille du Temple, cocktail of gay bars and chic cafes.

- Rue Oberkampf, Edgy urban hang-outs.

- Rue de Lappe, Boisterous Bastille bars and clubs.

- Rue de la Butte aux Cailles, Village atmosphere and fun local haunts.

Here are the cheapest places to drink:

Charlie and its two cents beer bar, which has a friendly atmosphere and offers a good selection of beers for just EUR2. This is a great place to hang out with friends. You can also go to the Irish pub, a bar in the Marais district. This is a popular place for students and offers a good happy hour.

Marlusse et lapin
This is a Hidden secret of Montmartre. They have a Good selection of Belgian beers for €5 each.

Address: 14 Rue Germain Pilon

Pop In · Bar

One of the friendliest places in Paris, home of the Parisian indie crowd. Cheap drinks and free gigs every night and entertaining open mic sessions on Sundays.

Address: 105 Rue Amelot

Zero Zero

Come here for happy hour drinks from 4 euros. There's a very small space for dancing which gets busy.

Address: 89 Rue Amelot

Le Viaduc

Located right by Gare de Lyon, they have almost everything on happy hour is 3€ and happy hour is every day 17h- 0200. There isn't another bar in Paris as cheap as this.

If you are looking for a wild night out, check out Rue de lappe and Rue de Mouffetard. Rue de lappe is located in Bastille and it's jammed packed with bars that's stay open all night, the party really never stops. Rue de Mouffetard is in the Latin Quarter it's slightly less wild, but its still a great time if you're trying to get your party on.

Drink along Rue Oberkampf

Close to canal St. Martin is Rue Oberkampf. Here you'll find a vibrant night scene. La Chat Noir has spoken word poetry (in English) one night a week so check it out. Plus there are shot bars, clubs, and great places to get cheap crepes for when you need a pick me up.

HISTORICAL INSIGHT: The cocktail was invented in Paris

The cocktail was invented in Paris, there are many different theories about how it came to be. Some believe that Henry Tepe invented the cocktail, while others think it was a creation of Harry MacElhone - his descendants continued to run Harry's Bar!

The Bloody Mary was created in Paris in Harry's New York Bar in 1921. Originally, it was named the Red Snapper, but later became the bloody mary. If you like cocktails pay a visit to Harry's Bar but with their experience comes a heavy pricetag.

Enjoy your first Day for under $20

Sculpture on the Arc de Triomphe

Start early, at the Eiffel Tower, Paris' most recognisable land-mark. After your selfies, stroll up the banks of the River Seine to Place de la Concorde. Enjoy views of the Champs Elysées and

LArc de Triomphe. Relax with some shop brought cheese and wine in Jardin du Carrousel, then visit one of the world's most famous museums, Museé du Louvre (free if you're under 26 and from the EU). After the Louvre walk down Rue de Rivoli. Turn onto Rue St. Martin and search for bargains in thrift stores. Just across the Seine on Ile de la Cité is where the Notre Dame Cathedral stands proud and this is a must-see even though it is being reconstructed after the fire. Walk back up to Place de la Concorde and stroll down the Champs Elyseés. Fill your belly at Breizh Café a delicious cheap creperie. At 10pm the Eiffel tower sparkles for 10 minutes and every hour after until 1am - don't miss it!

Itinerary if you're short of time

Please don't let people discourage you from seeing places because you don't have 2 weeks vacation time.

Day 1: climb the Eiffel Tower, roam the Parisian streets, enjoy the night time views of Eiffel Tower and carrousel then ate at a local cafe.
Day 2: visit the catacombs, La maison rose cafe, Sacré-Cœur Basilica, Arc De Triomphe and dinner at cafe del homme (so romantic).
Day 3: Photoshoot bright and early in the morning, breakfast at a cafe, The louvre and end your night with cabaret.

The Louvre is closed on Tuesdays So keep that in mind while planning your itinerary.

Basic Phrases

Parisan's on the whole do not like to speak English. And when you ask someone if they speak English, most will answer 'non'. Many say they a
strong
french accent and are shy of speaking English and others think it rude that tourists do not learn some basic French. Here are some Practical French phrases that are easy to remember to help you save money, make friends and avoid annoying the locals.

If you only remember one thing, Merci, which means thank you will be appreciated by servers.

Getting out of Paris cheaply

Bus

Flixbus
Booking flixbus journeys ahead can save you up to 98% of the cost of the ticket. You can visit lots of the favourite onward destinations such as Reims in France and further afield to Brussels for as little as $3 when you book six weeks in advance. flixbus.com

Car share
BlaBlaCar is a car sharing service commonly used in Paris - you can share a car to Brussels for $5 -
blablacar.com

Flights
At the time of Transavia are offering the cheapest flights onwards.Take advantage of discounts and specials. Sign up for e-newsletters from local carriers including Transavia to learn about special fares. Be careful with cheap airlines, most will allow hand-luggage only, and some charge for anything that is not a backpack. Check their websites before booking if you need to take luggage.

Airport Lounges

You don't need to be flying business or first class to enjoy an airport lounge. Here are three methods you can use to access lounges at Paris's airports:

- Get or use a credit card that gives free lounge access. NerdWallet has a good write-up about cards that offer free lounge access. www.nerdwallet.com/best/credit-cards/airport-lounge-access
- Buy onetime access. They start at $23 and often include free showers and free drinks and food.
- Find free access with the LoungeBuddy app. You pay an annual fee of $25 to use the app.

History of Paris

There's much to learn about Paris' history, from its Prehistoric inhabitants to the french revolution.

Prehistoric Paris

 Discovered in 2008 near Rue Henri-Farman in the 15th arrondissement are the oldest traces of human occupation in Paris. These remains belong to a hunter-gatherer encampment, dating to the Mesolithic period.

Prehistoric Paris was a river connecting to the Atlantic, with strategically placed islands providing shelter and protection. This river was a vital trade route, and its largest island attracted a Celtic tribe called the Parisii, who fished and traded along its banks in the 3rd century B.C.

Before Julius Ceasar arrived in 55BC, Paris was home to several thousand inhabitants. The island was alive with activity at that time, and the Parisii fought the Romans. They were eventually massacred by Roman troops, and the city was transformed into a Roman town. This new town was baptized Lutecia, and it remained that way for a few hundred years. The road that ran through the island is still in use today.

Enlightenment

In Paris, the Enlightenment was a time of social and intellectual reform. Though the French government tried to suppress it, private funding allowed new ideas to flourish. The Enlightenment ushered in a new era of scientific advancement and progress. The Enlightenment was defined by the ideas that were based on the principles of liberty, equality, and reason which still resound in Paris today.

Causes of the French Revolution

During the late 18th century, France was one of the most powerful countries in Europe. But there were deep divisions in society. In 1789, the country faced economic and food crises. This caused panic in Paris.

The monarchy was ruled by a weak and incompetent king, Louis XVI. This led to a wave of violence in Paris. The king had no interest in the welfare of the subjects. The king's autocratic rule was one of the major causes of the French Revolution. He was unable to address the need for tax reforms. His heavy tax burdens led to widespread resentment towards the monarchy. He was seen as inept and obscene.

The king failed to introduce a limited constitutional monarchy. He was also insensitive to the welfare of the lower classes. The monarchy was viewed as a wasteful institution.

The peasants revolted against the monarchy. They demanded equality and democratic rights. They also burned the homes of the aristocrats and tax collectors. These events led to a popular insurgency that culminated in the Storming of the Bastille.

The Place de la Concorde is the second largest square in France. This square was also known as the Place de la Revolution because it was the site of nearly 1,200 public beheadings during the French Revolution. Some of the most famous guillo-tine victims included King Louis XVI and Queen Marie Antoinette.

Napoleon's coup d'etat

Upon first glance, Napoleon's march on Paris was akin to a battle between the Nazis and the Soviets. ' It was the coup d'état that overthrew the system of government under the Directory in France and substituted the Consulate, making way for the despotism of Napoleon Bonaparte. The event is often viewed as the effective end of the French Revolution.;'

Haussmann's plan for modern Paris - 1853 and 1870

During the Second Empire, Baron Georges-Eugene Haussmann transformed Paris into a modern city. This was largely accomplished through ambitious urban renewal projects. He widened roads, rebuilt public buildings, and constructed a sewer system that channeled waste away from the city. He also commissioned new avenues and parks.

In the course of his plan, Haussmann demolished thousands of buildings. The city was overcrowded and dirty. He widened roads to accommodate the growing population. He also established a standard street width and height ratio. His plan also included new aqueducts, fountains, and lavatories.

Haussmann also reconstructed the last wing of the Louvre. He also reconstructed the Hotel-Dieu de Paris, which was situated on the Ile-de-la-Cite. He also commissioned the decorative band-stands that were installed in 27 parks. He also commissioned an impressive collection of street furniture.

Haussmann's work also included the construction of two new theaters, the Cirque Imperial and Theatre de la Ville. He also re-constructed the Place du Carousel, the last wing of the Louvre, and the Palais Garnier opera house.

Haussmann's legacy remains a complicated one. Patrice de Moncan, a French historian, says that he was "unjustly vil-lainized." She believes that Haussmann's work was actually beneficial to the health and wellbeing of Parisians. She says that the buildings built by Haussmann were stronger than those built by previous architects.

However, he also earned a reputation for social engineering. Thousands of low-income Parisians were forced to relocate to outer neighborhoods where the rents were lower. In addition, he was accused of destroying medieval treasures.

Avoid these tourist traps or scams

Scams and trickery are the scourge of a traveler's budget and unfortunately scams abound in Paris, and particularly near the attractions. Beware of extremely helpful strangers, distraction thefts are very common. If you are at all in doubt of someone's intention say 'No French, No English' and walk on. People can't con you if they can't speak to you.

'Found' Gold ring

A gypsy will offer you a found ring. Avoid this is a long-con.

Museum pickpockets

See the Mona Lisa without getting pickpocketed. Organised gangs operate around museum queues. Don't keep stuff in your back pockets and keep your bag where you can see it. Goes for using the metro too.

The string / bracelet scam

People will try to put a bracelet on you. If you let them weave it on your arm, they will tie it on so tight you won't be able to easily pull it off, and then they will demand money.

RECAP: How to have a $5,000 trip to Paris on a $500 budget

Find a cheap flight
Using the strategy we outlined you can snag a ticket to Paris from the states from $113 return. From the EU budget carrier Ryanair is flying to Paris from $5! Potential saving $1,000.

Blind book Five star hotels
The cheapest hotel deals are available when you 'blind book'. You don't know the name of the hotel before you book. Use Last Minute Top Secret hotels and you can find a four star hotel from $80 a night in Paris!
https://www.lastminute.com/hotels/france/paris/4-star-top-secret-hotel-in-paris

Pick-up delicious food
Install the 'Too Good To Go' app to get amazing food super cheap. Potential saving $150.

Restaurant deals / supermarket food / menu du jour
Nearly every restaurant in Paris offers a midday menu for lunch at around 12.90€ If you're on a budget, but like eating out, consider doing your dining in the daytime. Potential saving $500.

Book free tours
The best free tours fill up in advance. Book before you travel to save 150 dollars on tours.

Go to museums/ attractions on their free days
Get cultured for free, or for cheap, by knowing the gallery and museum discount days. The average traveller spends $300 on museums in Paris but there's no need to spend a dime if you time your trip to visit on the free days and or save money with the

Paris Museum Pass. Potential saving $300.

Drink outdoors with friends

Paris is super green and the best way to experience the city is to buy a bottle of wine from a supermarket and enjoy them somewhere green, or near the river. outdoor public spaces for a few drinks with friends. A wine costs around $8 in a bar. Potential savings on drinks $200 - hey you're on vacation! And thankfully there are no pesky open container laws in Paris.

Book Ahead
Book six weeks ahead for the lowest prices on outward buses and flights. Potential savings: $100

PRACTICAL THINGS TO REMEMBER TO SAVE MONEY IN PARIS

- Download google maps for for use offline.

- Book your Paris Greeters tour before you travel to start your trip with a free custom tour of Paris. Book any other free tours you wish to do.

- Download the French language pack on google translate - you will be grateful you have it! The camera function is great for translating French menus.

- Pick up food from the too good to go app - Plan to get your breakfast or dinner from restaurants on the app. $2.99 for a restaurant meal will save you at least $150 on the same delicious food in Paris. Boulangerie Utopie offers a magic bag of mixed pastries and cakes that would normally cost €12 for just €3 on the app.

- Know the names of Parisian foods to try and the star the restaurants to try them at on Google Maps.

- Go away from the main thoroughfare in Paris for cheaper restaurant prices

- Bring a good mosquito spray or combine a few drops of lemongrass oil with a moisturiser. This is the technique the Inca's used to keep mosquitos at bay. The smell turns the mosquitos around. Mosquitos are a pain in summertime.

- Pack food for the airport, you'll save $10 on a bad cup of coffee and stale croissant at the airport.

- Plan to start sightseeing early for a more serene experience.

- Avoid over-scheduling. You don't want to pack so much into your trip you wind up feeling like you're working on the conveyor belt called best sights of Paris instead of fully saturating your senses in the incredible sights, sounds, smells of the City of light.

Useful websites to save money

- https://www.discoverwalks.com/tour/city/Paris-walking-tours/ - free walking tour
- http://en.Parismuseumpass.com/ - entry to museums totalling $150 for $50
- https://www.ratp.fr/en/titres-et-tarifs/airport-tickets - bus to the airport $10
- https://www.thefork.com/best-promotions+Paris - restaurant deals
- https://www.gpsmycity.com/gps-tour-guides/Paris-488.html - self guided tours in Paris
- A weekly whats on written in English by locals. www.hipparis.com -

So there it is. You can save a small fortune by being strategic with your trip planning. We've arranged everything in the guide to offer the best bang for your buck. Which means we took the view that if it's not an excellent investment for your money, we wouldn't include it. Why would a guide called 'Super Cheap' include lots of overpriced attractions? That said, if you think we've missed something or have unanswered questions, ping me an email: philgtang@gmail.com I'm on central Europe time and usually reply within 8 hours of getting your mail. We like to think of our guide books as evolving organisms helping our readers travel better cheaper. We use reader questions via email to update this book year round so you'll be helping other readers and yourself.

Don't put your dreams off!

Time is a currency you never get back and travel is its greatest return on investment. Plus, now you know you can visit Paris for a fraction of the price most would have you believe.

Money Mistakes in Paris

Cost	Impact	Solution	Note
Using your home currency	Some credit card rates charge for every transaction in another currency. Check carefully before you use it	Use a prepaid currency card like Wise Multi-Currency Debit Card.	
Buying bottled water	At $2 a bottle, this is a cost that can mount up quickly	Refill from the tap. Bring an on the go water filter bottle like Water-to-go.	
Eating like a tourist	Eating at tourist traps can triple your bill. Choose wisely	Star cheap eats on google maps so you're never far from one	Tipping in France is not a way of life. Many restaurants and shops will include a service fee in the price of your meal, which means that you'll end up paying more than you need to.
Not agreeing a price of everything in advance	Taxi's and other unpriced services allow people to con you..	Agree the price beforehand to avoid unwanted bills or use ride hailing services.	
Not getting your VAT refund	20% of all sales purchases	super easy to do at the airport.	'After security, you can bring your Tax Free form validated By French Customs & passport to a Cash Paris or Travelex booth. You will receive your VAT refund in cash (€) or can have it transferred to your credit card which takes four to six weeks.'

The secret to saving HUGE amounts of money when travelling to Paris is...

Your mindset. Money is an emotional topic, if you associate words like cheapskate, Miser (and its £9.50 to go into Charles Dickens Paris house, oh the Irony) with being thrifty when travelling you are likely to say 'F-it' and spend your money needlessly because you associate pain with saving money. You pay now for an immediate reward. Our brains are prehistoric; they focus on surviving day to day. Travel companies and hotels know this and put trillions into making you believe you will be happier when you spend on their products or services. Our poor brains are up against outdated programming and an onslaught of advertisements bombarding us with the message: spending money on travel equals PLEASURE. To correct this carefully lodged propaganda in your frontal cortex, you need to imagine your future self.

Saving money does not make you a cheapskate. It makes you smart. How do people get rich? They invest their money. They don't go out and earn it; they let their money earn more money. So every time you want to spend money, imagine this: while you travel, your money is working for you, not you for money. While you sleep, the money, you've invested is going up and up. That's a pleasure a pricey entrance fee can't give you. Thinking about putting your money to work for you tricks your brain into believing you are not withholding pleasure from yourself, you are saving your money to invest so you can go to even more amazing places. You are thus turning thrifty travel into a pleasure fueled sport.

When you've got money invested - If you want to splash your cash on a first-class airplane seat - you can. I can't tell you how to invest your money, only that you should. Saving $20 on taxis doesn't seem like much, but over time you could save upwards of $15,000 a year, which is a deposit for a house which you can rent on Airbnb to finance more travel. Your brain making money looks like your brain on cocaine, so tell yourself saving money is making money.

Scientists have proved that imagining your future self is the easiest way to associate pleasure with saving money. You can download FaceApp — which will give you a picture of what you will look like older and grayer, or you can take a deep breath just before spending money and ask yourself if you will regret the purchase later.

The easiest ways to waste money traveling are:

Getting a taxi. The solution to this is to always download the google map before you go. Many taxi drivers will drive you around for 15 minutes when the place you were trying to get to is a 5-minute walk… remember while not getting an overpriced taxi to tell yourself, 'I am saving money to free myself for more travel.' Spending money on overpriced food when hungry. The solution: carry snacks. A banana and an apple will cost you, in most places, less than a dollar.

Spending on entrance fees to top-rated attractions. If you really want to do it, spend the money happily. If you're conflicted, sleep on it. I don't regret spending $200 on a sky dive over the Great Barrier Reef; I regret going to the top of the shard on a cloudy day in London for $60. Only you can know, but make sure it's your decision and not the marketing directors at said top-rated attraction.

Telling yourself 'you only have the chance to see/eat/experience it now'. While this might be true, make sure YOU WANT to spend the money. Money spent is money you can't invest, and often you can have the same experience for much less.

You can experience luxurious travel on a small budget, which will trick your brain into thinking you're already a high-roller, which will mean you'll be more likely to act like one and invest your money. Stay in five-star hotels for $5 by booking on the day of your stay on booking.com to enjoy last-minute deals. You can go to fancy restaurants using daily deal sites. Ask your airline about last-minute upgrades to first-class or business. I paid $100 extra on a $179 ticket to Cuba from Germany to be bumped to Business Class. When you ask, it will surprise you what you can get both at hotels and airlines.

Travel, as the saying goes, is the only thing you spend money on that makes you richer. You can easily waste money, making it difficult to enjoy that metaphysical wealth. The biggest money saving secret is to turn bargain hunting into a pleasurable activity, not an annoyance. Budgeting consciously can be fun, don't feel disappointed because you don't spend the $60 to go into an attraction. Feel good because soon that $60 will soon earn money for you. Meaning, you'll have the time and money to enjoy more metaphysical wealth while your bank balance increases.

Thank you for reading

Dear **Lovely Reader**,

If you have found this book useful, please consider writing a quick review on Amazon.

One person from every 1000 readers leaves a review on Amazon. It would mean more than you could ever know if you were one of our 1 in 1000 people to take the time to write a brief review.

Thank you so much for reading again and for spending your time and investing your trips future in Super Cheap Insider Guides. One last note, please don't listen to anyone who says 'Oh no, you can't visit Paris on a budget'. Unlike you, they didn't have this book. You can do ANYWHERE on a budget with the right insider advice and planning. Sure, learning to travel to Paris on a budget that doesn't compromise on anything or drastically compromise on safety or comfort levels is a skill, but this guide has done the detective work for you. Now it is time for you to put the advice into action.

Phil and the Super Cheap Insider Guides Team

P.S If you need any more super cheap tips we'd love to hear from you e-mail me at philgtang@gmail.com, we have a lot of contacts in every region, so if there's a specific bargain you're hunting we can help you find it.

DISCOVER YOUR NEXT VACATION

☑ **LUXURY ON A BUDGET APPROACH**
☑ **CHOOSE FROM 107 DESTINATIONS**
☑ **EACH BOOK PACKED WITH REAL-TIME LOCAL TIPS**

All are available in Paperback and e-book on Amazon: https://www.amazon.com/dp/B09C2DHQG5

Several are available as audiobooks. You can watch excerpts of ALL for FREE on YouTube: https://youtube.com/channel/UCxo9YV8-M9P1cFosU-Gjnqg

Super Cheap ADELAIDE 2023
Super Cheap ALASKA 2023
Super Cheap AMSTERDAM 2023
Super Cheap ANTIGUA 2023
Super Cheap ANTARCTICA 2023
Super Cheap AUSTIN 2023
Super Cheap BANGKOK 2023
Super Cheap BARBADOS 2023
Super Cheap BARCELONA 2023
Super Cheap BATH 2023
Super Cheap BELFAST 2023
Super Cheap BERMUDA 2023
Super Cheap BERLIN 2023
Super Cheap BIRMINGHAM 2023
Super Cheap BORA BORA 2023
Super Cheap BORDEAUX 2023
Super Cheap BRUGES 2023
Super Cheap BUDAPEST 2023
Super Cheap Bahamas 2023
Super Cheap Great Barrier Reef 2023

Super Cheap CABO 2023
Super Cheap CALGARY 2023
Super Cheap CAMBRIDGE 2023
Super Cheap CANCUN 2023
Super Cheap CAPPADOCIA 2023
Super Cheap CAPRI 2023
Super Cheap CARCASSONNE 2023
Super Cheap CHAMPAGNE REGION 2023
Super Cheap CHIANG MAI 2023
Super Cheap CHICAGO 2023
Super Cheap COPENHAGEN 2023
Super Cheap DOHA 2023
Super Cheap DOMINICAN REPUBLIC 2023
Super Cheap DUBAI 2023
Super Cheap DUBLIN 2023
Super Cheap EDINBURGH 2023
Super Cheap FLORENCE 2023
Super Cheap GALAPAGOS ISLANDS 2023
Super Cheap GALWAY 2023
Super Cheap HAVANA 2023
Super Cheap HELSINKI 2023
Super Cheap HONG KONG 2023
Super Cheap HONOLULU 2023
Super Cheap INNSBRUCK 2023
Super Cheap ISTANBUL 2023
Super Cheap KUALA LUMPUR 2023
Super Cheap LA 2023
Super Cheap LAPLAND 2023
Super Cheap LAS VEGAS 2023
Super Cheap LIMA 2023
Super Cheap LISBON 2023
Super Cheap LIVERPOOL 2023
Super Cheap LONDON 2023
Super Cheap MACHU PICHU 2023
Super Cheap MALAGA 2023

Super Cheap MALDIVES 2023
Super Cheap Machu Pichu 2023
Super Cheap MELBOURNE 2023
Super Cheap MIAMI 2023
Super Cheap MONACO 2023
Super Cheap Milan 2023
Super Cheap Munich 2023
Super Cheap NASHVILLE 2023
Super Cheap NEW ORLEANS 2023
Super Cheap NEW YORK 2023
Super Cheap NORWAY 2023
Super Cheap SAN FRANCISCO 2023
Super Cheap Santorini 2023
Super Cheap SEYCHELLES 2023
Super Cheap SINGAPORE 2023
Super Cheap SYDNEY 2023
Super Cheap ST LUCIA 2023
Super Cheap TORONTO 2023
Super Cheap TURKS AND CAICOS 2023
Super Cheap TURIN 2023
Super Cheap VENICE 2023
Super Cheap VIENNA 2023
Super Cheap WASHINGTON 2023
Super Cheap YORK 2023
Super Cheap YOSEMITE 2023
Super Cheap ZURICH 2023
Super Cheap ZANZIBAR 2023

Bonus Travel Hacks

I've included these bonus travel hacks to help you plan and enjoy your trip to Paris cheaply, joyfully, and smoothly. Perhaps they will even inspire you to start or renew a passion for long-term travel.

Common pitfalls when it comes to allocating money to <u>your desires</u> while traveling

Beware of Malleable mental accounting

Let's say you budgeted spending only $30 per day in Paris but then you say well if I was at home I'd be spending $30 on food as an everyday purchase so you add another $30 to your budget. Don't fall into that trap as the likelihood is you still have expenses at home even if its just the cost of keeping your freezer going.

Beware of impulse purchases in Paris

Restaurants that you haven't researched and just idle into can sometimes turn out to be great, but more often, they turn out to suck, especially if they are near tourist attractions. Make yourself a travel itinerary including where you'll eat breakfast and lunch. Dinner is always more expensive, so the meal best to enjoy at home or as a takeaway. This book is full of incredible cheap eats. All you have to do is plan to go to them.

Social media and FOMO (Fear of Missing Out)

'The pull of seeing acquaintances spend money on travel can often be a more powerful motivator to spend more while traveling than seeing an advertisement.' Beware of what you allow to influence you and go back to the question, what's the best money I can spend today?

Now-or-never sales strategies

One reason tourists are targeted by salespeople is the success of the now-or-never strategy. If you don't spend the money now... your never get the opportunity again. Rarely is this true.

Instead of spending your money on something you might not actually desire, take five minutes. Ask yourself, do I really want this? And return to the answer in five minutes. Your body will either say an absolute yes with a warm, excited feeling or a no with a weak, obscure feeling.

Unexpected costs

"Holding on to anger is like grasping a hot coal with the intent of throwing it at someone else; you only hurt yourself." The Buddha.

One downside to traveling is unexpected costs. When these spring up from airlines, accommodation providers, tours and on and on, they feel like a punch in the gut. During the pandemic my earnings fell to 20% of what they are normally. No one was traveling, no one was buying travel guides. My accountant out of nowhere significantly raised his fee for the year despite the fact there was a lot less money to count. I was so angry I consulted a lawyer who told me you will spend more taking him to court than you will paying his bill. I had to get myself into a good feeling place before I paid his bill, so I googled how to feel good paying someone who has scammed you.

The answer: Write down that you will receive 10 times the amount you are paying from an unexpected source. I did that. Four months later, the accountant wrote to me. He had applied for a COVID subsidy for me and I would receive… you guessed it almost exactly 10 times his fee.

Make of that what you want. I don't wish to get embroiled in a conversation about what many term 'woo-woo', but the result of my writing that I would receive 10 times the amount made me feel much, much better when paying him. And ultimately, that was a gift in itself. So next time some airline or train operator or hotel/ Airbnb sticks you with an unexpected fee, immediately write that you will receive 10 times the amount you are paying from an unexpected source. Rise your vibe and skip the added price of feeling angry.

Hack your allocations for your Paris Trip

"The best trick for saving is to eliminate the decision to save." Perry Wright of Duke University.

Put the money you plan to spend in Paris on a pre-paid card in the local currency. This cuts out two problems - not knowing how much you've spent and totally avoiding expensive currency conversion fees.

You could even create separate spaces. This much for transportation, this for tours/entertainment, accommodation and food. We are reluctant to spend money that is pre-assigned to categories or uses.

Write that you want to enjoy a $3,000 trip for $500 to your Paris trip. Countless research shows when you put goals in writing, you have a higher chance of following through.

Spend all the money you want to on buying experiences in Paris

"Experiences are like good relatives that stay for a while and then leave. Objects are like relatives who move in and stay past their welcome." Daniel Gilbert, psychologist from Harvard University.

Economic and psychological research shows we are happier buying brief experiences on vacation rather than buying stuff to wear so give yourself freedom to spend on experiences knowing that the value you get back is many many times over.

Make saving money a game

There's one day a year where all the thrift shops where me and my family live sell everything there for a $1. My wife and I hold a contest where we take $5 and buy an entire outfit for each other. Whoever's outfit is liked more wins. We also look online to see whose outfit would have cost more to buy new. This year, my wife even snagged me an Armani coat for $1. I liked the coat when she showed it to me, but when I found out it was $500 new; I liked it and wore it a lot more.

Quadruple your money

Every-time you want to spend money, imagine it quadrupled. So the $10 you want to spend is actually $40. Now imagine that what you want to buy is four times the price. Do you still want it? If yes, go enjoy. If not, you've just saved yourself money, know you can choose to invest it in a way that quadruples or allocate it to something you really want to give you a greater return.

Understand what having unlimited amounts of money to spend in Paris actually looks like

Let's look at what it would be like to have unlimited amounts of money to spend on your trip to Paris.

Isolation

You take a private jet to your private Paris hotel. There you are lavished with the best food, drink, and entertainment. Spending vast amounts of money on vacation equals being isolated.

If you're on your honeymoon and you want to be alone with your Amore, this is wonderful, but it can be equally wonderful to make new friends. Know this a study 'carried out by Brigham Young University, Utah found that while obesity increased risk of death by 30%, loneliness increased it by half.'

Comfort

Money can buy you late check outs of five-star hotels and priority boarding on airlines, all of which add up to comfort. But as this book has shown you, saving money in Paris doesn't minimize comfort, that's just a lie travel agencies littered with glossy brochures want you to believe.

You can do late-check outs for free with the right credit cards and priority boarding can be purchased with a lot of airlines from $4. If you want to go big with first-class or business, flights offset your own travel costs by renting your own home or you can upgrade at the airport often for a fraction of what you would have paid booking a business flight online.

MORE TIPS TO FIND CHEAP FLIGHTS

"The use of travelling is to regulate imagination by reality, and instead of thinking how things may be, to see them as they are." Samuel Jackson

If you're working full-time, you can save yourself a lot of money by requesting your time off from work starting in the middle of the week. Tuesdays and Wednesdays are the cheapest days to fly. You can save thousands just by adjusting your time off.

The simplest secret to booking cheap flights is open parameters. Let's say you want to fly from Chicago to Paris. You enter the USA in from and select France under to. You may find flights from New York City to Paris for $70. Then you just need to find a cheap flight to NYC. Make sure you calculate full costs, including if you need airport accommodation and of course getting to and from airports, **but in nearly every instance open parameters will save you at least half the cost of the flight.**

If you're not sure about where you want to go, use open parameters to show you the cheapest destinations from your city. Start with skyscanner.net they include the low-cost airlines that others like Kayak leave out. Google Flights can also show you cheap destinations. To see these leave the WHERE TO section blank.

Open parameters can also show you the cheapest dates to fly. If you're flexible, you can save up to 80% of the flight cost. Always check the weather at your destination before you book. Sometimes a $400 flight will be $20, because it's monsoon season. But hey, if you like the rain, why not?

ALWAYS USE A PRIVATE BROWSER TO BOOK FLIGHTS

Skyscanner and other sites track your IP address and put prices up and down based on what they determine your strength of conviction to buy. e.g. if you've booked one-way and are looking for the return, these sites will jack the prices up by in most cases 50%. Incognito browsing pays.

Use a VPN such as Hola to book your flight from your destination

Install Hola, change your destination to the country you are flying to. The location from which a ticket is booked can affect the price significantly as algorithms consider local buying power.

Choose the right time to buy your ticket.

Choose the right time to buy your ticket, as purchasing tickets on a Sunday has been proven to be cheaper. If you can only book during the week, try to do it on a Tuesday.

Mistake fares

Email alerts from individual carriers are where you can find the best 'mistake fares". This is where a computer error has resulted in an airline offering the wrong fare. In my experience, it's best to sign up to individual carriers email lists, but if you ARE lazy Secret Flying puts together a daily roster of mistake fares. Visit https://www.secretflying.com/errorfare/ to see if there're any errors that can benefit you.

Fly late for cheaper prices

Red-eye flights, the ones that leave later in the day, are typically cheaper and less crowded, so aim to book that flight if possible. You will also get through the airport much quicker at the end of the day. Just make sure there's ground transport available for when you land. You don't want to save $50 on the airfare and spend it on a taxi to your accommodation.

Use this APP for same day flights

If your plans are flexible, use 'Get The Flight Out' (http://www.gtfoflights.com/) a fare tracker Hopper that shows you same-day deeply discounted flights. This is best for long-haul flights with major carriers. You can often find a British Airways round-trip from JFK Airport to Heathrow for $300. If you booked this in advance, you'd pay at least double.

Take an empty water bottle with you

Airport prices on food and drinks are sky high. It disgusts me to see some airports charging $10 for a bottle of water. ALWAYS take an empty water bottle with you. It's relatively unknown, but most airports have drinking water fountains past the security check. Just type in your airport name to wateratairports.com to locate the fountain. Then once you've passed security (because they don't allow you to take 100ml or more of liquids) you can freely refill your bottle with water.

Round-the-World (RTW) Tickets

It is always cheaper to book your flights using a DIY approach. First, you may decide you want to stay longer in one country, and a RTW will charge you a hefty fee for changing your flight. Secondly, it all depends on where and when you travel and as we have discussed, there are many ways to ensure you pay way less than $1,500 for a year of flights. If you're travelling long-haul, the best strategy is to buy a return ticket, say New York, to Bangkok and then take cheap flights or transport around Asia and even to Australia and beyond.

Cut your costs to and from airports

Don't you hate it when getting to and from the airport is more expensive than your flight! And this is true in so many cities, especially European ones. For some reason, Google often shows the most expensive options. Use Omio to compare the cheapest transport options and save on airport transfer costs.

Car sharing instead of taxis

Check if Paris has car sharing at the airport. Often they'll be tons of cars parked at the airport that are half the price of taking a taxi into the city. In most instances, you register your driving licence on an app and scan the code on the car to get going.

Checking Bags

Sometimes you need to check bags. If you do, put an Air-Tag inside. That way, you'll be about to see when you land where your bag is. This saves you the nail biting wait at baggage claim. And if worse comes to worst, and you see your bag is actually in another city, you can calmly stroll over to customer services and show them where your bag is.

Is it cheaper and more convenient to send your bags ahead?

Before you check your bags, check if it's cheaper to send them ahead of you with sendmybag.com obviously if you're staying in an Airbnb, you'll need to ask the hosts permission or you can time them to arrive the day after you. Hotels are normally very amenable.

What Credit Card Gives The Best Air Miles?

You can slash the cost of flights just for spending on a piece of plastic.

LET'S TALK ABOUT DEBT

Before we go into the best cards for each country, let's first talk about debt. The US system offers the best and biggest rewards. Why? Because they rely on the fact that many people living in the US will not pay their cards in full and the card will earn the bank significant interest payments. Other countries have a very different attitude towards money, debt, and saving than Americans. Thus in Germany and Austria the offerings aren't as favourable as the UK, Spain and Australia, where debt culture is more widely embraced. The takeaway here is this: **Only spend on one of these cards when you have set-up an automatic total monthly balance repayment. Don't let banks profit from your lizard brain!**

The best air-mile credit cards for those living in the UK

Amex Preferred Rewards Gold comes out top for those living in the UK for 2023.

Here are the benefits:

- 20,000-point bonus on £3,000 spend in first three months. These can be used towards flights with British Airways, Virgin Atlantic, Emirates and Etihad, and often other rewards, such as hotel stays and car hire.

- 1 point per £1 spent
- 1 point = 1 airline point
- Two free visits a year to airport lounges
- No fee in year one, then £140/yr

The downside:

- Fail to repay fully and it's 59.9% rep APR interest, incl fee

You'll need to cancel before the £140/yr fee kicks in year two if you want to avoid it.

The best air-mile credit cards for those living in Canada

Aeroplan is the superior rewards program in Canada. The card has a high earn rate for Aeroplan Points, generating 1.5 points per $1 spent on eligible purchases. Look at the specifics of the eligible purchases https://www.aircanada.com/ca/en/aco/home/aeroplan/earn.html. If you're not spending on these things AMEX's Membership Rewards program offers you the best returns in Canada.

The best air-mile credit cards for those living in Germany

If you have a German bank account, you can apply for a Lufthansa credit card.

Earn 50,000 award miles if you spend $3,000 in purchases and paying the annual fee, both within the first 90 days.

Earn 2 award miles per $1 spent on ticket purchases directly from Miles & More integrated airline partners.

Earn 1 award mile per $1 spent on all other purchases.

The downsides

the €89 annual fee

Limited to fly with Lufthansa and its partners but you can capitalise on perks like the companion pass and airport lounge vouchers.

You need excellent credit to get this card.

The best air-mile credit cards for those living in Austria

"In Austria, Miles & More offers you a special credit card. You get miles for each purchase with the credit card. The Miles & More program calculates miles earned based on the distance flown and booking class. For European flights, the booking class is a flat rate. For intercontinental flights, mileage is calculated by multiplying the booking class by the distance flown." They offer a calculator so you can see how many points you could earn: https://www.miles-and-more.com/at/en/earn/airlines/mileage-calculator.html

The best air-mile credit cards for those living in Spain:

"The American Express card is the best known and oldest to earn miles, thanks to its membership Rewards program. When making payments with this card, points are added, which can then be exchanged for miles from airlines such as Iberia, Air Europa, Emirates or Alitalia." More information is available here: https://www.americanexpress.com/es-es/

The best air-mile credit cards for those living in Australia

ANZ Rewards Black comes out top for 2023.

180,000 bonus ANZ Reward Points (can get an $800 gift card) and $0 annual fee for the first year with the ANZ Rewards Black
Points Per Spend: 1 Velocity point on purchases of up to $5,000 per statement period and 0.5 Velocity points thereafter.
Annual Fee: $0 in the first year, then $375 after.

Ns no set minimum income required, however, there is a minimum credit limit of $15,000 on this card.

Here are some ways you can hack points onto this card: https://www.pointhacks.com.au/credit-cards/anz-rewards-black-guide/

The best air-mile credit card solution for those living in the USA with a POOR credit score

The downside to Airline Mile cards is that they require good or excellent credit scores, meaning 690 or higher.

If you have bad credit and want to use credit card air lines you will need to rebuild your credit poor. The Credit One Bank® Platinum Visa® for Rebuilding Credit is a good credit card for people with bad credit who don't want to place a deposit on a secured card. The Credit One Platinum Visa offers a $300 credit limit, rewards, and the potential for credit-limit increases, which in time will help rebuild your score.

PLEASE don't sign-up for any of these cards if you can't trust yourself to repay it in full monthly. This will only lead to stress for you.

Frequent Flyer Memberships

"Points" and "miles" are often used interchangeably, but they're usually two very different things. Maximise and diversify your rewards by utilising both.

A frequent-flyer program (FFP) is a loyalty program offered by an airline. They are designed to encourage airline customers to fly more to accumulate points (also called miles, kilometres, or segments) which can be redeemed for air travel or other rewards.

You can sign up with any FFP program for free. There are three major airline alliances in the world: Oneworld, Sky-Team and Star Alliance. I am with One World https://www.oneworld.com/members because the points can be accrued and used for most flights.

The best return on your points is to use them for international business or first class flights with lie-flat seats. You would need 3 times more miles compared to an economy flight, but if you paid cash, you'd pay 5 - 10 times more than the cost of the economy flight, so it really pays to use your points only for upgrades. The worst value for your miles is to buy an economy seat or worse, a gift from the airlines gift-shop.

Sign up for a family/household account to pool miles together. If you share a common address, you can claim the miles with most airlines. You can use AwardWallet to keep track of your miles. Remember that they only last for 2 years, so use them before they expire.

How to get 70% off a Cruise

An average cruise can set you back $4,000. If you dream of cruising the oceans, but find the pricing too high, look at repositioning cruises. You can save as much as 70% by taking a cruise which takes the boat back to its home port.

These one-way itineraries take place during low cruise seasons when ships have to reposition themselves to locations where there's warmer weather.

To find a repositioning cruise, go to vacationstogo.com/repositioning_cruises.cfm. This simple and often overlooked booking trick is great for avoiding long flights with children and can save you so much money!

It's worth noting we don't have any affiliations with any travel service or provider. The links we suggest are chosen based on our experience of finding the best deals.

Pack like a Pro

"He who would travel happily must travel light." – Antoine de St. Exupery 59.

Travel as lightly as you can. We always need less than we think. You will be very grateful that you have a light pack when changing trains, travelling through the airport, catching a bus, walking to your accommodation, or climbing stairs.

Make a list of what you will wear for 7 days and take only those clothes. You can easily wash your things while you're travelling if you stay in an Airbnb with a washing machine or visit a local laundrette. Roll your clothes for maximum space usage and fewer wrinkles. If you feel really nervous about travelling with such few things, make sure you have a dressier outfit, a little black dress for women is always valuable, a shirt for men. Then pack shorts, a long pair of pants, loose tops and a hoodie to snuggle in. Remind yourself that a lack of clothing options is an opportunity to find bargain new outfits in thrift stores. You can either sell these on eBay after you've worn them or post them home to yourself. You'll feel less stressed, as you don't have to look after or feel weighed down by excess baggage. Here are three things to remember when packing:

- Co-ordinate colours - make sure everything you bring can be worn together.

- Be happy to do laundry - fresh clothes when you're travelling feels very luxurious.

- Take liquid minis no bigger than 60ml. Liquid is heavy, and you simply don't need to carry so much at one time.

- Buy reversible clothes (coats are a great idea), dresses which can be worn multiple different ways.

Checks to Avoid Fees

Always have 6 months' validity on your passport

To enter most countries, you need 6 months from the day you land. Factor in different time zones around the world if your passport is on the edge. Airport security will stop you from boarding your flight at the airport if your passport has 5 months and 29 days left.

Google Your Flight Number before you leave for the airport

Easily find out where your plane is from anywhere. Confirm the status of your flight before you leave for the airport with flightaware.com. This can save you long unnecessary wait times.

Check-in online

The founder, Ryan O'Leary of budget airline Ryanair famously said: "We think they should pay €60 for [failing to check-in online] being so stupid.". Always check-in online, even for international flights. Cheaper international carriers like Scoot will charge you at the airport to check-in.

Checking Bags

Never, ever check a bag if you can avoid it. Sometimes you need to check bags. If you do, put an AirTag inside. That way, you'll be about to see when you land where your bag is. This saves you the nail biting wait at baggage claim. And if worse comes to worst, and you see your bag is actually in another city, you can calmly stroll over to customer services and show them where your bag is.

Is it cheaper and more convenient to send your bags ahead?

Before you check your bags, check if it's cheaper to send them ahead of you with <u>sendmybag.com</u> obviously if you're staying in an Airbnb, you'll need to ask the hosts permission or you can time them to arrive the day after you. Hotels are normally very amenable.

It is always cheaper to put heavier items on a ship, rather than take them on a flight with you. Find the best prices for shipping at <u>https://www.parcelmonkey.com/delivery-services/shipping-heavy-items</u>

Use a fragile sticker

Put a 'Fragile' sticker on anything you check to ensure that it's handled better as it goes through security. It'll also be one of the first bags released after the flight, getting you out of the airport quicker.

If you check your bag, photograph it

Take a photo of your bag before you check it. This will speed up the paperwork if it is damaged or lost.

Relaxing at the Airport

The best way to relax at the airport is in a lounge where they provide free food, drinks, comfortable chairs, luxurious amenities (many have showers) and, if you're lucky, a peaceful ambience. If you're there for a longer time, look for Airport Cubicles, sleep pods which charge by the hour.

You can use your FFP Card (Frequent Flyer Memberships) to get into select lounges for free. Check your eligibility before you pay.

If you're travelling a lot, I'd recommend investing in a <u>Priority Pass</u> for the airport.

It includes 850-plus airport lounges around the world. The cost is $99 for the year and $27 per lounge visit or you can pay $399 for the year all inclusive.

If you need a lounge for a one-off day, you can get a Day Pass. Buy it online for a discount, it always works out cheaper than buying at the airport. Use <u>www.Lounge-Pass.com</u>.

Lounges are also great if you're travelling with kids, as they're normally free for kids and will definitely cost you less than snacks for your little ones. The rule is that kids should be seen and not heard, so consider this before taking an overly excited child who wants to run around, or you might be asked to leave even after you've paid.

How to spend money

Bank ATM fees vary from $2.50 per transaction to as high as $5 or more, depending on the ATM and the country. You can completely skip those fees by paying with card and using a card which can hold multiple currencies.

Budget travel hacking begins with a strategy to spend without fees. Your individual strategy depends on the country you legally reside in as to what cards are available. Happily there are some fin-tech solutions which can save you thousands on those pesky ATM withdrawal fees and are widely available globally. Here are a selection of cards you can pre-charge with currency for Paris:

N26

N26 is a 12-year-old digital bank. I have been using them for over 6 years. The key advantage is fee-free card transactions abroad. They have a very elegant app, where you can check your timeline for all transactions listed in real time or manage your in-app security anywhere. The card you receive is a Mastercard so you can use it everywhere. If you lose the card, you don't have to call anyone, just open the app and swipe 'lock card'. It puts your purchases into a graph automatically so you can see what you spend on. You can open an account from abroad entirely online, all you need is your passport and a camera n26.com

Revolut

Revolut is a multi-currency account that allows you to hold and exchange 29 currencies and spend fee-free abroad. It's a UK based neobank, but accepts customers from all over the world.

  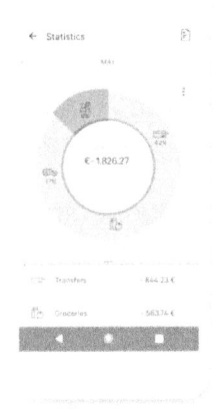

Wise debit card

If you're going to be in one place for a long time, the Wise debit card is like having your travel money on a card – it lets you spend money at the real exchange rate.

Monzo

Monzo is good if your UK based. They offer a fee-free UK account. Fee-free international money transfers and fee-free spending abroad.

The downside

The cards above are debit cards, meaning you need to have money in those accounts to spend it. This comes with one big downside: safety. Credit card issuers' have "zero liability" meaning you're not liable for unauthorised charges. All the cards listed above do provide cover for unauthorised charges but times vary greatly in how quickly you'd get your money back if it were stolen.

The best option is to check in your country to see which credit cards are the best for travelling and set up monthly payments to repay the whole amount so you don't pay unnecessary interest. In the USA, Schwab regularly ranks at the top for travel credit cards. Credit cards are always the safer option when abroad simply because you get your money back faster if its stolen and if you're renting cars, most will give you free insurance when you book the car rental using the card, saving you money.

Always withdraw money; never exchange.

Money exchanges, whether they be on the streets or in the airports will NEVER give you a good exchange rate. Do not bring bundles of cash. Instead, withdraw local currency from the ATM as needed and try to use only free ATMs. Many in airports charge you a fee to withdraw cash. Look for bigger ATMs attached to banks to avoid this.

Recap

- Take cash from local, non-charging ATMs for the best rates.

- Never change at airport exchange desks unless you absolutely have to, then just change just enough to be able get to a bank ATM.

- Bring a spare credit card for emergencies.

- Split cash in various places on your person (pockets, shoes) and in your luggage. It's never sensible to keep your cash or cards all in one place.

- In higher risk areas, use a money belt under your clothes or put $50 in your shoe or bra.

Revolut

Revolut is a multi-currency account that allows you to hold and exchange 29 currencies and spend fee-free abroad. It's a UK based neobank, but accepts customers from all over the world.

Wise debit card
If you're going to be in one place for a long time the Wise debit card is like having your travel money on a card – it lets you spend money at the real exchange rate.

Monzo
Monzo is good if your UK based. They offer a fee-free UK account. Fee-free international money transfers and fee-free spending abroad.

The downside

The cards above are debit cards, meaning you need to have money in those accounts to spend it. This comes with one big downside: safety. Credit card issuers' have "zero liability" meaning you're not liable for unauthorised charges. All of the cards listed above do provide cover for unauthorised charges but times vary greatly in how quickly you'd get your money back if it were stolen.

The best option is to check in your country to see which credit cards are the best for travelling and set up monthly payments to repay the whole amount so you don't pay unnecessary interest. In the USA, Schwab[2] regularly ranks at the top for travel credit cards. Credit cards are always the safer option when abroad simply because you get your money back faster if its stolen and if you're renting cars, most will give you free insurance when you book the car rental using the card, saving you money.

---

[2] Charles Schwab High Yield Checking accounts refund every single ATM fee worldwide, require no minimum balance and have no monthly fee.

Always withdraw money; never exchange.

Money exchanges whether they be on the streets or in the airports will NEVER give you a good exchange rate. Do not bring bundles of cash. Instead withdraw local currency from the ATM as needed and try to use only free ATM's. Many in airports charge you a fee to withdraw cash. Look for bigger ATM's attached to banks to avoid this.

Recap

- Take cash from local, non-charging ATMs for the best rates.
- Never change at airport exchange desks unless you absolutely have to, then just change just enough to be able get to a bank ATM.
- Bring a spare credit card for emergencies.
- Split cash in various places on your person (pockets, shoes) and in your luggage. Its never sensible to keep your cash or cards all in one place.
- In higher risk areas, use a money belt under your clothes or put $50 in your shoe or bra.

How to save money while travelling

Saving money while travelling sounds like an oxymoron, but it can be done with little to no effort. Einstein is credited as saying, "Compound interest is the eighth wonder of the world." If you saved and invested $100 today, in 20 years, it would be $2,000 thanks to the power of compound interest. It makes sense then to save your money, invest and make even more money.

The Acorns app is a simple system for this. It rounds up your credit card purchases and puts the rest into a savings account. So if you pay for a coffee and its $3.01, you'll save 0.99 cents. You won't even notice you're saving by using this app: www.acorns.com

Here are some more generic ways you can always save money while travelling:

Device Safety

Having your phone, iPad or laptop stolen is one BIG and annoying way you can lose money travelling. The simple solution is to use apps to track your devices. Some OSes have this feature built-in. Prey will try your smartphones or laptops (preyproject.com).

Book New Airbnb's

When you take a risk on a new Airbnb listing, you save money. Just make sure the hosts profile is at least 3 years old and has reviews.

If you end up in an overcrowded city

The website https://campspace.com/ is like Airbnb for camping in people's garden and is a great way to save money if you end up in a city during a big event.

Look out for free classes

Lots of hostels offer free classes for guests. If you're planning to stay in a hostel, check out what classes your hostel offers. I have learnt languages, cooking techniques, dance styles, drawing and all manner of things for free by taking advantage of free classes at hostels.

Get student discounts

If you're studying buy an ISIC card - International Student Identity Card. It is internationally recognised, valid in 133 countries and offers more than 150,000 discounts!

Get Senior Citizen discounts

Most state run attractions, ie, museums, galleries will offer a discount for people over 65 with ID.

Instal maps.me

Maps me is extremely good for travelling without data. It's like offline google maps without the huge download size.

Always buy travel insurance

Don't travel without travel insurance. It is a small cost to pay compared with what could be a huge medical bill.

Travel Apps That'll Make Budget Travel Easier

Travel apps are useful for booking and managing travel logistics. They have one fatal downside: they can track you in the app and keep prices up. If you face this, access the site from an incognito browser tab.

Here are the best apps and what they can do for you:

- Best For flight Fare-Watching: Hopper.

- Best for booking flights: Skyscanner and Google Flights

- Best for timing airport arrivals: FlightAware - check on delays, cancellations and gate changes.

- Best for overcoming a fear of flying: SkyGuru - turbulence forecasts for the route you're flying.

- Best for sharing your location: TripWhistle - text or send your GPS coordinates or location easily.

- Best for splitting expenses among co-travellers: Splittr, Trip Splitter, Venmo or Splitwise.

How NOT to be ripped off

"One of the great things about travel is that you find out how many good, kind people there are."
— Edith Wharton

The quote above may seem ill placed in a chapter entitled how not to be ripped off, but I included it to remind you that the vast majority of people do not want to rip you off. In fact, scammers are normally limited to three situations:

1. Around heavily visited attractions - these places are targeted purposively due to sheer footfall. Many criminals believe ripping people off is simply a numbers game.

2. In cities or countries with low-salaries or communist ideologies. If they can't make money in the country, they seek to scam foreigners. If you have travelled to India, Morocco or Cuba you will have observed this phenomenon.

3. When you are stuck and the person helping you know you have limited options.

Scammers know that most people will avoid confrontation. Don't feel bad about utterly ignoring someone and saying no. Here are six strategies to avoid being ripped off:

1. **Never ever agree to pay as much as you want. Always decide on a price before.**

Whoever you're dealing with is trained to tell you, they are uninterested in money. This is a trap. If you let people do this they will ask for MUCH MORE money at the end, and because you have used there service, you will feel obliged to pay. This is a conman's trick and nothing more.

2. Pack light

You can move faster and easier. If you take heavy luggage, you will end up taking taxis which are comparatively very costly over time.

3. NEVER use the airport taxi service. Plan to use public transport before you reach the airport.

4. Don't buy a sim card from the airport. Buy from the local supermarkets it will cost 50% less.

5. Eat at local restaurants serving regional food

Food defines culture. Exploring all delights available to the palate doesn't need to cost enormous sums.

6. **Ask the locals what something should cost,** and try not to pay over that.

7. **If you find yourself with limited options.** e.g. your taxi dumps you on the side of the road because you refuse to pay more (common in India and parts of South America) don't act desperate and negotiate as if you have other options or you will be extorted.

8. Don't blindly rely on social media[3]

Let's say you post in a Facebook group that you want tips for travelling to The Maldives. A lot of the comments you will receive come from guides, hosts and restaurants doing their own promotion. It's estimated that 50% or more of

---

[3] https://arstechnica.com/tech-policy/2019/12/social-media-platforms-leave-95-of-reported-fake-accounts-up-study-finds/

Facebook's current monthly active users are fake. And what's worse, a recent study found Social media platforms leave 95% of reported fake accounts up. These accounts are the digital versions of the men who hang around the Grand Palace in Bangkok telling tourists its closed, to divert you to shops where they will receive a commission for bringing you.

It can also be the case that genuine comments come from people who have totally different interests, beliefs and yes, budgets to yours. Make your experience your own and don't believe every comment you read.

Bottom line: use caution when accepting recommendations on social media and always fact-check with your own research.

Small tweaks on the road add up to big differences in your bank balance

Take advantage of other hotel amenities

If you fancy a swim but you're nowhere near the ocean, try the nearest hotel with a pool. As long as you buy a drink, the hotel staff will probably grant you access.

Fill up your mini bar for free.

Fill up your mini bar for free by storing things from the breakfast bar or grocery shop in your mini bar to give you a greater selection of drinks and food without the hefty price tag.

Save yourself some ironing

Use the steam from the shower to get rid of wrinkles in clothing. If something is creased, leave it trapped with the steam in the bathroom overnight for even better results.

See somewhere else for free

Opt for long stopovers, allowing you to experience another city without spending much money.

Wear your heaviest clothes

On the plane to save weight in your pack, allowing you to bring more with you. Big coats can then be used as pillows to make your flight more comfortable.

Don't get lost while you're away.

Find where you want to go using Google Maps, then type 'OK Maps' into the search bar to store this information for offline viewing.

Use car renting services

Share Now or Car2Go allow you to hire a car for 2 hours for $25 in a lot of European countries.

Share Rides

Use sites like blablacar.com to find others who are driving in your direction. It can be 80% cheaper than normal transport. Just check the drivers reviews.

Use free gym passes

Get a free gym day pass by googling the name of a local gym and free day pass.

When asked by people providing you a service where you are from..

If there's no price list for the service you are asking for, when asked where you are from, Say you are from a lesser-known poorer country. I normally say Macedonia, and if they don't know where it is, add it's a poor country. If you say UK, USA, the majority of Europe bar the well-known poorer countries taxi drivers, tour operators etc will match the price to what they think you pay at home.

Set-up a New Uber/ other car hailing app account for discounts

By googling you can find offers with $50 free for new users in most cities for Uber/ Lyft/ Bolt and alike. Just set up a new gmail.com email account to take advantage.

Where and How to Make Friends

"People don't take trips, trips take people." – John Steinbeck

Become popular at the airport

Want to become popular at the airport? Pack a power bar with multiple outlets and just see how many friends you can make. It's amazing how many people forget their chargers, or who packed them in the luggage that they checked in.

Stay in Hostels

First of all, Hostels don't have to be shared dorms, and they cater to a much wider demographic than is assumed. Hostels are a better environment for meeting people than hotels, and more importantly, they tended to open up excursion opportunities that further opened up that opportunity.

Or take up a hobby

If hostels are a definite no-no for you; find an interest. Take up a hobby where you will meet people. I've dived for years and the nature of diving is you're always paired up with a dive buddy. I met a lot of interesting people that way.

Small tweaks on the road add up to big differences in your bank balance

Take advantage of other hotel's amenities

If you fancy a swim but you're nowhere near the ocean, try the nearest hotel with a pool. As long as you buy a drink, the hotel staff will likely grant you access.

Fill up your mini bar for free.

Fill up your mini bar for free by storing things from the breakfast bar or grocery shop in your mini bar to give you a greater selection of drinks and food without the hefty price tag.

Save yourself some ironing

Use the steam from the shower to get rid of wrinkles in clothing. If something is creased, leave it trapped with the steam in the bathroom overnight for even better results.

See somewhere else for free

Opt for long stopovers, allowing you to experience another city without spending much money.

Wear your heaviest clothes

on the plane to save weight in your pack, allowing you to bring more with you. Big coats can then be used as pillows to make your flight more comfortable.

Don't get lost while you're away.

Find where you want to go using Google Maps, then type 'OK Maps' into the search bar to store this information for offline viewing.

Use car renting services

Share Now or Car2Go allow you to hire a car for 2 hours for $25 in a lot of Europe.

Share Rides

Use sites like blablacar.com to find others who are driving in your direction. It can be 80% cheaper than normal transport. Just check the drivers reviews.

Use free gym passes

Get a free gym day pass by googling the name of a local gym and free day pass.

When asked by people providing you a service where you are from..

If there's no price list for the service you are asking for, when asked where you are from, Say you are from a lesser-known poorer country. I normally say Macedonia, and if they don't know where it is, add it's a poor country. If you say UK, USA, the majority of Europe bar the well-known poorer countries taxi drivers, tour operators etc will match the price to what they think you pay at home.

Set-up a New Uber/ other car hailing app account for discounts

By googling you can find offers with $50 free for new users in most cities for Uber/ Lyft/ Bolt and alike. Just set up a new gmail.com email account to take advantage.

Where and How to Make Friends

"People don't take trips, trips take people." – John Steinbeck

Become popular at the airport

Want to become popular at the airport? Pack a power bar with multiple outlets and just see how many friends you can make. It's amazing how many people forget their chargers, or who packed them in the luggage that they checked in.

Stay in Hostels

First of all, Hostels don't have to be shared dorms, and they cater to a much wider demographic than is assumed. Hostels are a better environment for meeting people than hotels, and more importantly they tended to open up excursion opportunities that further opened up that opportunity.

Or take up a hobby

If hostels are a definite no-no for you; find an interest. Take up a hobby where you will meet people. I've dived for years and the nature of diving is you're always paired up with a dive buddy. I met a lot of interesting people that way.

When unpleasantries come your way...

We all have our good and bad days travelling, and on a bad day you can feel like just taking a flight home. Here are some ways to overcome common travel problems:

Anxiety when flying

It has been over 40 years since a plane has been brought down by turbulence. Repeat that number to yourself: 40 years! Planes are built to withstand lighting strikes, extreme storms and ultimately can adjust course to get out of their way. Landing and take-off are when the most accidents happen, but you have statistically three times the chance of winning a huge jackpot lottery, then you do of dying in a plane crash.

If you feel afraid on the flight, focus on your breathing saying the word 'smooth' over and over until the flight is smooth. Always check the airline safety record on airlinerating.com I was surprised to learn Ryanair and Easyjet as much less safe than Wizz Air according to those ratings because they sell similarly priced flights. If there is extreme turbulence, I feel much better knowing I'm in a 7 star safety plane.

Wanting to sleep instead of seeing new places

This is a common problem. Just relax, there's little point doing fun things when you feel tired. Factor in jet-lag to your travel plans. When you're rested and alert you'll enjoy your new temporary home much more. Many people hate the first week of a long-trip because of jet-lag and often blame this on their first destination, but its rarely true. Ask travellers who 'hate' a particular place and you will see that very often they either had jet-lag or an unpleasant journey there.

Going over budget

Come back from a trip to a monster credit card bill? Hopefully, this guide has prevented you from returning to an unwanted bill. Of course, there are costs that can creep up and this is a reminder about how to prevent them making their way on to your credit card bill:

- To and from the airport. Solution: leave adequate time and take the cheapest method - book before.

- Baggage. Solution: take hand luggage and post things you might need to yourself.

- Eating out. Solution: go to cheap eats places and suggest those to friends.

- Parking. Solution: use apps to find free parking

- Tipping. Solution Leave a modest tip and tell the server you will write them a nice review.

- Souvenirs. Solution: fridge magnets only.

- Giving to the poor. (This one still gets me, but if you're giving away $10 a day - it adds up) Solution: volunteer your time instead and recognise that in tourist destinations many beggars are run by organised crime gangs.

Price v Comfort

I love traveling. I don't love struggling. I like decent accommodation, being able to eat properly and see places and enjoy. I am never in the mood for low-cost airlines or crappy transfers, so here's what I do to save money.

- Avoid organised tours unless you are going to a place where safety is a real issue. They are expensive and constrain your wanderlust to typical things. I only recommend them in Algeria, Iran and Papua New Guinea - where language and gender views pose serious problems all cured by a reputable tour organiser.

- Eat what the locals do.

- Cook in your Airbnb/ hostel where restaurants are expensive.

- Shop at local markets.

- Spend time choosing your flight, and check the operator on arilineratings.com

- Mix up hostels and Airbnbs. Hostels for meeting people, Airbnb for relaxing and feeling 'at home'.

Not knowing where free toilets are

Use Toilet Finder - https://play.google.com/store/apps/details?id=com.bto.toilet&hl=en

Your Airbnb is awful

Airbnb customer service is notoriously bad. Help yourself out. Try to sort things out with the host, but if you can't, take photos of everything e.g bed, bathroom, mess, doors, contact them within 24 hours. Tell them you had to leave and pay for new accommodation. Ask politely for a full refund including booking fees. With photographic evidence and your new accommodation receipt, they can't refuse.

The airline loses your bag

Go to the Luggage desk before leaving the airport and report the bag missing. Hopefully you've headed the advice to put an AirTag in your checked bag and you can show them where to find your bag. Most airlines will give you an overnight bag, ask where you're staying and return the bag to you within three days. It's extremely rare for Airlines to lose your bag due to technological innovation, but if that happens you should submit an insurance claim after the three days is up, including receipts for everything you had to buy in the interim.

Your travel companion lets you down

Whether it's a breakup or a friend cancelling, it sucks and can ramp up costs. The easiest solution to finding a new travel companion is to go to a well-reviewed hostel and find someone you want to travel with. You should spend at least three days getting to know this person before you suggest travelling together. Finding someone in person is always better than finding someone online, because you can get a better idea of whether you will have a smooth journey together. Travel can make or break friendships.

Culture shock

I had one of the strongest culture shocks while spending 6 months in Japan. It was overwhelming how much I had to prepare when I went outside of the door (googling words and sentences what to use, where to go, which station and train line to use, what is this food called in Japanese and how does its look etc.). I was so tired constantly but in the end I just let go and went with my extremely bad Japanese. If you feel culture shocked its because your brain is referencing your surroundings to what you know. Stop comparing, have Google translate downloaded and relax.

Your Car rental insurance is crazy expensive

I always use <u>carrentals.com</u> and book with a credit card. Most credit cards will give you free insurance for the car, so you don't need to pay the extra. Some unsavoury companies will bump the price up when you arrive. Ask to speak to a manager. If this doesn't resolve, it google "consumer ombudsman for NAME OF COUNTRY." and seek an immediate full refund on the balance difference you paid. It is illegal in most countries to alter the price of a rental car when the person arrives to pickup a pre-arranged car.

A note on Car Rental Insurance

Always always always rent a car with a credit card that has rental vehicle coverage built into the card and is automatically applied when you rent a car. Then there's no need to buy additional rental insurance (check with your card on the coverage they protect some exclude collision coverage). Do yourself a favour when you step up to the desk to rent the car tell the agent you're already covered and won't be buying anything today. They work on commission and you'll save time and your patience avoiding the upselling.

You're sick

First off ALWAYS, purchase travel insurance. Including emergency transport up to $500k even to back home, which is usually less than $10 additional. I use <u>https://www.comparethemarket.com/travel-insurance/</u> to find the best days. If I am sick I normally check into a hotel with room service and ride it out.

Make a Medication Travel Kit

Take travel sized medications with you:

- Antidiarrheal medication (for example, bismuth sub-salicylate, loperamide)

- Medicine for pain or fever (such as acetaminophen, aspirin, or ibuprofen)

- Throat Lozenges

Save yourself from most travel related hassles

- Do not make jokes with immigration and customs staff. A misunderstanding can lead to HUGE fines.

- Book the most direct flight you can find nonstop if possible.

- Carry a US$50 bill for emergency cash. I have entered a country and all ATM and credit card systems were down. US$ can be exchanged nearly anywhere in the world and is useful in extreme situations, but where possible don't exchange, as you will lose money.

- Check, and recheck, required visas and such BEFORE the day of your trip. Some countries, for instance, require a ticket out of the country in order to enter. Others, like the US and Australia, require electronic authorisation in advance.

- Airport security is asinine and inconsistent around the world. Keep this in mind when connecting flights. Always leave at least 2 hours for international connections or international to domestic. In Stansted for example, they force you to buy one of their plastic bags, and remove your liquids from your own plastic bag…. just to make money from you. And this adds to the time it will take to get through security, so lines are long.

- Wiki travel is perfect to use for a lay of the land.

- Expensive luggage rarely lasts longer than cheap luggage, in my experience. Fancy leather bags are toast with air travel.

Food

- When it comes to food, eat in local restaurants, not tourist-geared joints. Any place with the menu in three or more languages is going to be overpriced.

- Take a spork - a knife, spoon and fork all in one.

Water Bottle

Take a water bottle with a filter. We love these ones from Water to Go.

Empty it before airport security and separate the bottle and filter as some airport people will try and claim it has liquids…

Bug Sprays

If you're heading somewhere tropical spray your clothes with Permethrin before you travel. It lasts 40 washes and saves space in your bag. A 'Bite Away' zapper can be used after the bite to totally erase it. It cuts down on the itching and erases the bite from your skin.

Order free mini's

Don't buy those expensive travel sized toiletries, order travel sized freebies online. This gives you the opportunity to try brands you've never used before, and who knows, you might even find your new favourite soap.

Take a waterproof bag

If you're travelling alone you can swim without worrying about your phone, wallet and passport laying on the beach.

You can also use it as a source of entertainment on those ultra budget flights.

Make a private entertainment centre anywhere

Always take an eye-mask, earplugs, a scarf and a kindle reader - so you can sleep and entertain yourself anywhere!

The best Travel Gadgets

The door alarm

If you're nervous and staying in private rooms or airbnbs take a door alarm. For those times when you just don't feel safe, it can help you fall asleep. You can get tiny ones for less than $10 from Amazon: https://www.amazon.com/Travel-door-alarm/s?k=Travel+door+alarm

Smart Blanket

Amazon sells a 6 in 1 heating blanket that is very useful for cold plane or bus trips. Its great if you have poor circulation as it becomes a detachable Foot Warmer: Amazon http://amzn.to/2hTYlOP I paid $49.00.

The coat that becomes a tent

https://www.adiff.com/products/tent-jacket. This is great if you're going to be doing a lot of camping.

Clever Tank Top with Secret Pockets

Keep your valuables safe in this top. Perfect for all climates. https://www.amazon.com/Clever-Travel-Companion-Unisex-secret/dp/B00O94PXLE on Amazon for $39.90

Optical Camera Lens for Smartphones and Tablets

Leave your bulky camera at home. Turn your device into a high-performance camera. Buy on Amazon for $9.95

Travel-sized Wireless Router with USB Media Storage

Convert any wired network to a wireless network. Buy on Amazon for $17.99

Buy a Scrubba Bag to wash your clothes on the go

Or a cheaper imitable. You can wash your clothes on the go.

Hacks for Families

Rent an Airbnb apartment so you can cook

Apartments are much better for families, as you have all the amenities you'd have at home. They are normally cheaper per person too. We are the first travel guide publisher to include Airbnb's in our recommendations if you think any of these need updating you can email me at philgtang@gmail.com

Shop at local markets

Eat seasonal products and local products. Get closer to the local market and observe the prices and the offer. What you can find more easily, will be the cheapest.

Take Free Tours

Download free podcast tours of the destination you are visiting. The podcast will tell you where to start, where to go, and what to look for. Often you can find multiple podcast tours of the same place. Listen to all of them if you like, each one will tell you a little something new.

Pack Extra Ear Phones

If you go on a museum tour, they often have audio guides. Instead of having to rent one for each person, take some extra earphones. Most audio tour devices have a place to plug in a second set.

Buy Souvenirs Ahead of Time

If you are buying souvenirs somewhere touristy, you are paying a premium price. By ordering the same exact products online, you can save a lot of money.

Use Cheap Transportation

Do as the locals do, including weekly passes.

Carry Reusable Water Bottles

Spending money on water and other beverages can quickly add up. Instead of paying for drinks, take some refillable water bottles.

Combine Attractions

Many major cities offer ticket bundles where one price gets you into 5 or 6 popular attractions. You will need to plan ahead of time to decide what things you plan to do on vacation and see if they are selling these activities together.

Pack Snacks

Granola bars, apples, baby carrots, bananas, cheese crackers, juice boxes, pretzels, fruit snacks, apple sauce, grapes, and veggie chips.

Stick to Carry-On Bags

Do not pay to check a large bag. Even a small child can pull a carry-on.

Visit free art galleries and museums

Just google the name + free days.

Eat Street Food

There's a lot of unnecessary fear around this. You can watch the food prepared. Go for the stands that have a steady queue.

Travel Gadgets for Families

Dropcam

Are what-if scenarios playing out in your head? Then you need Dropcam.

'Dropcam HD Internet Wi-Fi Video Monitoring Cameras help you watch what you love from anywhere. In less than a minute, you'll have it setup and securely streaming video to you over your home Wi-Fi. Watch what you love while away with Dropcam HD.'

Approximate Price: $139

Kelty-Child-Carrier

Voted as one of the best hiking essentials if you're traveling with kids and can carry a child up to 18kg.

Jetkids Bedbox

No more giving up your own personal space on the plane with this suitcase that becomes a bed.

Safety

"If you think adventure is dangerous, try routine. It's lethal." – Paulo Coelho

Backpacker murdered is a media headline that leads people to think traveling is more dangerous than it is. The media sensationalise the rare murders and deaths of backpackers and travellers. The actual chances of you dying abroad are extremely extremely low.

Let's take the USA as an example. In 2018, 724 Americans **died** from unnatural causes, 167 died from car accidents, while the majority of the other deaths resulted from drownings, suicides, and non-vehicular accidents. Contrast this with the 15,000 murders in the US in 2018, and travelling abroad looks much safer than staying at home.

There are many things you can to keep yourself safe. Here are our tips.

1. Always check fco.co.uk before travelling. NEVER RELY on websites or books. Things are changing constantly and the FCO's (UK's foreign office) advice is always UP TO DATE (hourly) and **extremely conservative**.

2. Check your mindset. I've travelled alone to over 180 countries and the main thing I learnt is if you walk around scared, or anticipating you're going to be pickpocketed, your constant fear will attract bad energy. Murders or attacks on travellers are the mainstay of media, not reality, especially in countries familiar with travellers. The only place I had cause to genuinely fear for my life was Papua New Guinea -

where nothing actually happened to me only my own panic over culture shock.

There are many things you can do to stop yourself being victim to the two main problems when travelling: theft or being scammed.

I will address theft first. Here are my top tips:

- Stay alert while you're out and always have an exit strategy.

- Keep your money in a few different places on your person and your passport somewhere it can't be grabbed.

- Take a photo of your passport on your phone in case. If you do lose it, google for your embassy, you can usually get a temporary pretty fast.

- Google safety tips for travelling in your country to help yourself out and memorise the emergency number.

- At hostels, keep your large bag in the room far under the bed/out of the way with a lock on the zipper.

- On buses/trains, I would even lock my bag to the luggage rack.

- Get a personal keychain alarm. The sound will scare anyone away.

- Don't wear any jewellery. A man attempted to rob a friend of her engagement ring in Bogota, Colombia, and in hindsight I wished I'd told her to leave it at home/wear it on a hidden necklace, as the chaos it created was avoidable.

- Don't turn your back to traffic while you use your phone.

- When travelling in the tuktuk sit in the middle and keep your bag secure. Wear sunglasses as dust can easily get in your eyes.

- Don't let anyone give you flowers, bracelets, or any type of trinket, even if they insist it's for free and compliment you like crazy.

- Don't let strangers know that you are alone - unless they are travel friends ;-)

- Lastly, and most importantly -Trust your gut! If it doesn't feel right, it isn't.

How I got hooked on budget travelling

'We're on holiday' is what my dad used to say to justify getting us in so much debt we lost our home and all our things when I was 11. We moved from the suburban bliss of Hemel Hempstead to a run down council estate in inner-city London, near my dad's new job as a refuge collector, a fancy word for dustbin man. I lost all my school friends while watching my dad go through a nervous breakdown.

My dad loved walking up a hotel lobby desk without a care in the world. So much so, that he booked overpriced holidays on credit cards. A lot of holidays. As it turned out, we couldn't afford any of them. In the end, my dad had no choice but to declare bankruptcy. When my mum realised, he'd racked up so much debt our family unit dissolved. A neat and perhaps as painless a summary of events that lead me to my life's passion: budget travel that doesn't compromise on fun, safety or comfort.

I started travelling full-time at the age of 18. I wrote the first Super Cheap Insider guide for friends visiting Norway - which I did for a month on less than $250. When sales reached 10,000 I decided to form the Super Cheap Insider Guides company. As I know from first-hand experience debt can be a noose around our necks, and saying 'oh come on, we're on vacation' isn't a get out of jail free card. In fact, its the reverse of what travel is supposed to bring you - freedom.

Before I embarked upon writing Super Cheap Insider guides, many, many people told me that my dream was impossible. Travelling on a budget could never be comfortable. I hope this guide has proved to you what I have known for a long-time: budget travel can feel luxurious when you know and use the insider hacks.

And apologies if I depressed you with my tale of woe. My dad is now happily remarried and works as a chef in London at a fancy hotel - the kind he used to take us to!

A final word...

There's a simple system you can use to think about budget travel. In life, we can choose two of the following: cheap, fast, or quality. So if you want it Cheap and fast you will get a lower quality service. Fast-food is the perfect example. The system holds true for purchasing anything while travelling. I always choose cheap and quality, except at times where I am really limited on time. Normally, you can make small tweaks to make this work for you. Ultimately, you must make choices about what's most important to you and heed your heart's desires.

'Your heart is the most powerful muscle in your body. Do what it says.' Jen Sincero

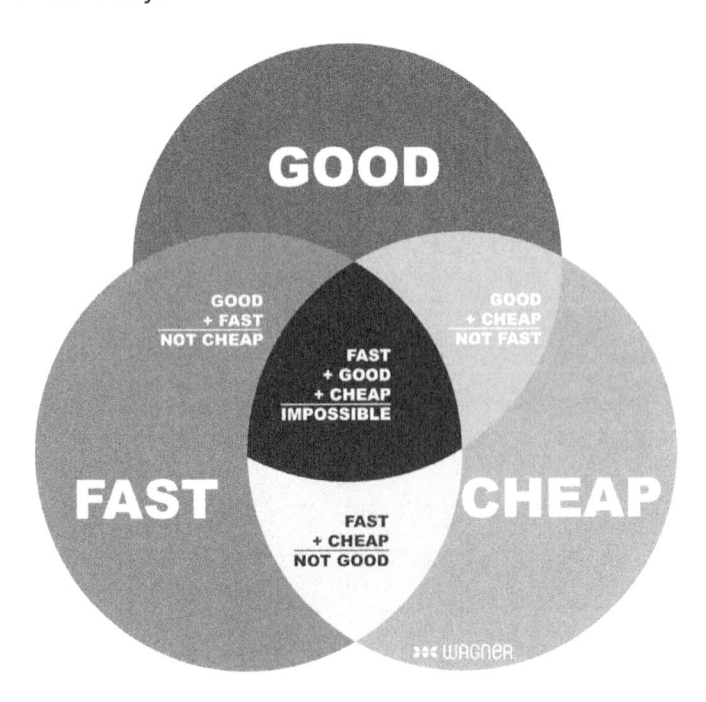

Our Writers

Phil Tang was born in London to Irish immigrant, Phil graduated from The London School of Economics with a degree in Law. Now he travels full-time in search of travel bargains with his wife, dog and a baby and a toddler.

Ali Blythe has been writing about amazing places for 17 years. He loves travel and especially tiny budgets equalling big adventures nearly as much as his family. He recently trekked the Satopanth Glacier trekking through those ways from where no one else would trek. Ali is an adventurer by nature and bargainist by religion.

Michele Whitter writes about languages and travel. What separates her from other travel writers is her will to explain complex topics in a no-nonsense, straightforward way. She doesn't promise the world. But always delivers step-by-step methods you can immediately implement to travel on a budget.

Lizzy McBraith, Lizzy's input on Super Cheap Insider Guides show you how to stretch your money further so you can travel cheaper, smarter, and with more wanderlust. She loves going over land on horses and helps us refine each guide to keep them effective. **If you've found this book useful, please consider leaving a short review on Amazon. it would mean a lot.Copyright**

If you've found this book useful, please select five stars on Amazon. Knowing I helped you save money in Paris would mean genuinely make my day.

Copyright

Printed in Great Britain
by Amazon